1P4

0390

D1022069

A Rock and A Hard Place
Inside Canada's Parole Board

Lisa Hobbs Birnie

Macmillan of Canada
A Division of Canada Publishing Corporation Limited
Toronto, Ontario, Canada

Canadian Cataloguing in Publication Data

Lisa Hobbs Birnie, date.
  A rock and a hard place : inside Canada's Parole Board

ISBN 0-7715-9418-6

1. Canada.   National Parole Board.
2. Parole — Canada.   I. Title

HV9308.B57 1990   364.6'2'0971   C89-090674-2

1 2 3 4 5 ARC 94 93 92 91 90

Cover design by Don Fernley

Macmillan of Canada
A Division of Canada Publishing Corporation
Toronto, Ontario, Canada

Printed and bound in the United States

Contents

Foreword

At the time I was asked to serve on the National Parole Board, I was on the editorial staff of the *Vancouver Sun*. As a career journalist for over twenty-five years, I had travelled a fair bit and had observed first-hand some of the major political and social upheavals of our times. Now in mid-life, I was ready for a change, and when the offer to join the board came in 1978, I accepted with cheerful ignorance and an open mind.

I was curious to find out what the board was all about. I was already aware that, although the public held strong and usually negative opinions about its workings, few people knew anything about the board, its organization, processes, and membership, or about the laws and regulations under which it operated. Nor did they know much about Correctional Service Canada, which is responsible for prison inmates sentenced to two years or more.

When I joined the board I decided to take things as I found them, to make my own judgement about its problems, and, I hoped, to contribute to its effectiveness. Always a writer, in the back of my mind I imagined I might find material in my experiences for a book.

Once on the board, I entered a world more complicated, disturbing, fascinating, heart-rending, infuriating, and exhausting than anything I could have imagined.

The work of the National Parole Board is important, difficult, and grossly misunderstood. My task in this book has been to explain how the board works, and to illustrate the human context within which it functions, mainly through looking at specific cases of what happens to prisoners and their families before, during and after a parole hearing. I have attempted to record objectively my personal experiences as a member of the board from February, 1978, to June, 1986, in the hope that they will cast light on the board's operations and its success in fulfilling its mandate to release eligible inmates back into society when, in the board's judgement, these inmates are unlikely to reoffend or endanger the public.

Being a board member, I soon found out, meant participating daily in human dramas that repeatedly touch on key issues of justice and law. These issues are far more complex than they seem to the general public and their resolution, if there is one, involves not only the board and the offender, but also parole officers, correctional staff, victims, psychologists and psychiatrists, judges, community representatives, and the police.

The perception of the board as a group of misguided and moderately dull-witted political pork-barrellers who capriciously pull their decisions out of thin air remains dear to many people, and whose opinions are based mainly on the "bad" decisions made by the board. As there is little public interest in stories of inmates who become responsible citizens, only the "bad" decisions are publicized by the media, even though government processes that were once secret are now open to public scrutiny, under the Charter of Rights and Freedoms.

The board's decisions are not made in a vacuum; they are influenced by many factors, such as the inmate's criminal history, the availability or lack of rehabilitative programs, the inmate's attitude to his offence, and the degree to which he has community support. To understand the work of the board it is necessary to have some appreciation of prisons, of the effect and availability of rehabilitation programs, of the effects of the Canadian Charter of Rights and Freedoms, of specific types of offences and offenders, and of a myriad of other problems.

In the three years since I left the board some things have

changed. The most important change has come about from Bills C-67 and C-68, the so-called "Detention Legislation" that went into effect on July 24, 1986. This gave the board the power to keep certain dangerous inmates in prison after they had reached their mandatory supervision date — so-called "gating". Previously, all inmates were automatically released when they reached this date, which is set at the completion of two-thirds of the sentence. This legislation also requires the board to interview each inmate when he has served one-sixth of his time, as well as at his full parole eligibility date, set at one-third of all sentences.

There have been other changes since I left. For instance, the regulations that govern the board's mandate under the Parole Act (1958) have been amended; the criteria for granting or denying parole have been more specifically spelled out; the relationships between the National Parole Board and the provincial parole boards in Ontario and British Columbia have radically changed; and the number of members who vote on specific cases has been reduced, while the number of temporary members — part-time members called in to assist full-time members when the board is overloaded — has been increased. Of the members with whom I worked during my tenure, half remain on the board at the time of this writing, while the other half have retired or have left because their appointments were not renewed.

While these changes mean that some new appointees are carrying out some new processes, the problems that board members and inmates must work out when they face each other across a prison desk remain the same, a fact that was evident when I attended board hearings as an observer in August, 1989. Although the rights of individuals are now far more clearly defined than before and are enshrined in the Charter, the dilemmas that a releasing agency such as the board must resolve are little different today from what they were when the ticket-of-leave system was developed in Australia in the early 1800s, or when "An Act To Provide for the Conditional Liberation of Convicts" was passed by the Canadian Parliament in 1899. The need to protect society, the need to be fair to inmates, and the difficulty of predicting human behaviour — especially after exposure to the destructive effects of prison — pose the same challenges to the board that society itself has always faced.

I have read that the word "parole" was first used in 1846, but the concept of prisoners being able to gain a pardon after serving some of their time has existed since 1617, when an Order of the English Privy Council sent convicts to the New World as indentured servants where, with time, they could purchase their freedom. Thus, the idea of conditional liberation is not an experimental notion dreamed up by pious liberals in recent times. It has a long history, and has managed to survive for four hundred years in the climate of ongoing tension between law and justice, and between the good of the individual and the good of society.

When I joined the board my ideas on the subject of crime and criminals were rather academic. I had never been a victim of crime nor had anyone close to me. I was curious about the forces that formed a criminal lookout — family background, poverty, greed, and so on — but I had little feeling for the actual people involved and limited insight into the issues. I did, however, have strong views about prisons. As a reporter I'd visited many of them, mainly in the United States and Australia, but also in Canada. It was clear to me that prisons provided the illusion of public safety while creating a unique underclass, a segregated welfare state that implicitly elevated the rest of us who did not belong to it.

As I travelled across the country and the years passed, my attitudes towards crime and the individuals involved in it changed. Sometimes I try to retrace these early years to see why I softened here, hardened there. When did I start having to repress an angry despair over child abusers and their frequent accomplices — the children's mothers? When did I start to think of alcohol as poison and marijuana as less harmful? Was there one particular case that made me an advocate of a national native parole board to handle native cases? Was there one police report or the accumulated thousands I read that turned me into a vigorous defender of the police, despite the presence of a few fascists and bullies among them? Was it the third, or fifth, or tenth case of wife murder reduced to manslaughter that made me realize how deeply rooted in our society is the idea of women as chattels? When was it that my heart started to pound, my hands go clammy on entering an underground parking-lot at night?

And when was it that I began to recognize the anger of many inmates as profound grief, the despair and longing of a small neglected child? Or faced the unsettling fact that the more I saw of contract killers and members of organized crime the less sure I was of my anti-capital punishment views? When was it that I recognized as much hate in myself as I found in some of the inmates, or found more sensitivity in some of the inmates than existed in some of the board members?

I don't know. I do know that I learned very quickly that to identify myself socially as a member of the parole board was to give a signal for a barrage to begin. "What the hell were you people thinking about, letting So-and-so out?" or "How many rapists did you let out this week?" were common reactions from otherwise pleasant people in otherwise pleasant gatherings. It was useless, I found, to suggest that the board did not make its decisions by spinning a wheel, nor did we receive mysterious phone calls from mysterious people "at the top" who directed our voting in the "big" cases.

Dostoyevsky once said that the ultimate proof of being human was the ability to commit an idiotic act. This axiom came to my mind often during parole hearings, not only in relation to an inmate's foolish actions, but also in relation to the mistakes society has made and continues to make when dealing with offenders. The resulting financial and human cost is now too high for these mistakes to be allowed to continue.

For purposes of anonymity and confidentiality, all cases used in this book (excluding those referred to in legal documents in the discussion of the Charter of Rights and Freedoms in Chapter 3) are fictitious. The names of inmates and their family members are fictitious, as are their backgrounds, occupations, offences, and sentences. The names of cities and towns, of penitentiaries, institutions, and halfway houses are real. The names of organizations that work within prisons, such as Alcoholics Anonymous or Native Clan, are real. All hearings and all conversations are fictionalized accounts of what might normally be said.

Because I worked only occasionally in the Prison for Women at Kingston and at Tanguay Prison for Women, its francophone counterpart in Montreal, and dealt with male inmates 95 percent of my time, I have used "he" to describe inmates throughout the book.

Finally, I talked with many different people who have somehow been involved in Canada's justice and correctional systems. However, the views expressed are my own and not necessarily endorsed by any of them.

Lisa Hobbs Birnie
September, 1989

Acknowledgements

Many people contributed to the writing of this book and I am deeply grateful to every one of them. Their generosity with their time and their willingness to share their specialized knowledge, as well as their views regarding the criminal justice system, helped me greatly. I would particularly like to thank the Hon. Mr. Justice James K. Hugessen, of the Federal Court of Appeal of Canada; and Mr. Justice H.D. Parker, and Mr. Justice Gerald C. King, both of the Provincial Court of Saskatchewan, for their encouragement. I would also like to thank John Conroy for his assistance with the section on the Charter of Rights and Freedoms; psychologist Mike Webster; Sylvia Griffiths of the John Howard Society, and the unfailingly helpful librarians at the B.C. Courthouse Library, University of British Columbia Law Library, and the sociology department of the Vancouver City Library.

Most of all I want to thank Betty Lou Edwards, consultant, for her constructive help and boundless generosity in sharing with me her specialized knowledge of the criminal justice system.

My final note of thanks is to Wilf Birnie, for his time, patience, and immeasurable support and assistance.

Acronyms

AA – Alcoholics Anonymous

AADAC – Alcohol and Drug Addiction Centre

B&E – Break and Enter

CSC – Correction Service Canada

LUDO – Living Unit Development Officer – now usually called Case Management Officer (institutional) – a member of the prison staff who works with the inmate to develop a schedule of activities and acts as the prisoner's liaison with the administration. The LUDO assesses the inmate's attitude and performance during imprisonment and reports details to the Parole Board hearing.

MAP – Matsqui Alcohol Program

MS – Mandatory Supervision – an inmate must be released on MS by law after serving two-thirds of a non-life sentence, provided that behaviour in prison has been acceptable and parole has not already been granted.

NA – Narcotics Anonymous

PC – Protective Custody – inmates may be put in PC while in prison, for their own protection from other inmates. This can involve being locked up for 23 1/2 hours per day.

PFV – Private Family Visit – are of a duration of forty-eight hours every two months or twenty-four hours every month. However, the frequency and time available varies from institution to institution due to space shortage and the large number of inmates and families requesting PFVs. There is no period of eligibility but practical limitations often preclude participation until at least six months after incarceration.

PO – Parole Officer – this is the inmate's link with the community. The PO acts as the inmate's supervisor after release on parole and is responsible for ensuring that the inmate has suitable support in the community. This involves interviewing the inmate, his family and prospective employers (if any), and reporting details to the Parole Board hearing.

Parole supervision on the street involves: for medium to high-risk inmates – face-to-face contact no less than four times per month; for low-risk inmates, face-to-face contact twice a month for the first six months, once a month from six months to twelve months and once every two months after twelve months. The categorization of an inmate as "high risk" or "low risk" is done by the CSC.

RPC – Regional Psychiatric Centre

TA – Temporary Absence – can be either unescorted temporary absence (UTA) or escorted temporary absence (ETA). There is a minimum six-month waiting period, or one-sixth of sentence, before an inmate (except lifers) becomes eligible for a UTA. A UTA is granted mainly for home visits, halfway house visits, and employment or study purposes. An ETA means that an unarmed peace officer or person hired by CSC is responsible for taking an inmate to his destination and returning him to the institution. Most ETAs are to visit medical specialists or to appear in court. Except for lifers, decisions regarding ETAs are made by the Warden.

1 *Baptism by Fire*

I attended my first National Parole Board hearing in Drumheller, a mean and miserable medium-security prison set in the badlands northeast of Calgary. The cases I heard in these first two days on the board were like hundreds of other miserable tragedies that I was to witness over the next eight years. What I most remember is not so much their specific details, but rather the overall chaos of the process of which I was now to be a part. I was the neophyte, there to observe how the other two experienced board members conducted hearings, how they addressed inmates, and how they obtained the information they needed to decide whether or not and how an inmate should be released.

The hearing-room located in the administration centre was nothing special, just a medium-sized room furnished with a scattering of wooden chairs and one oversized desk. At one end of the desk sat a prison staff member with reports on the inmate's institutional behaviour: at the other end was the parole officer who would supervise the inmate on the street if the board granted parole.

The first case was that of Bobbie John Roth. He had been born in Inverness, Alberta, of an unknown father and an alcoholic mother. He was removed from his mother by child protection authorities when he was two and placed in a series of foster homes, staying in some for up to two years, in others for a matter of weeks. He started drinking heavily at twelve and had been drinking at the time of the current offences: forcible confinement, and break-and-enter and commit. He had been on his own since age sixteen and for the past two years — he was now nineteen — he had used cocaine and marijuana regularly. He claimed to have completed grade eight but the prison staff had noticed that he had difficulty reading. Roth wrote no letters in jail and he received none, nor did he have any visitors. Immature for his age, he could not get along with other inmates, particularly with natives, whom he seemed to despise. Drumheller's population was 20 percent native and 10 percent Métis. Two months earlier Roth had been severely beaten by a group of native prisoners.

Before he was beaten, he had regularly attended Alcoholics Anonymous meetings. A report from Ron Belan, an outside volunteer who ran the prison's AA program, said Roth was beginning to understand his alcohol and drug addiction, and that this had encouraged the inmate to put his name on the waiting-list for academic upgrading courses offered in the prison. However, following the beating, he had requested protective custody (PC) and still remained there. As a result of being in PC, which meant spending twenty-three and a half hours a day in lockup, he was unable to attend either the AA meetings or upgrading courses. He had requested a hearing with the board to gain a day parole so that he could attend an Alcohol and Drug Addiction Centre (AADAC) called Recovery Acres. After completing this course he planned to enroll in a cooking course at Alberta Vocational College in Calgary. He had no savings, no work skills, and no community support other than the AADAC.

His offences had occurred in February, 1976. Roth received five years for break-and-enter and commit and four concurrent years for forcible confinement, which meant a total sentence of five years. The sentence became effective in June, 1976, with a day-parole eligibility date of April, 1977; a full-parole eligibility date of February, 1978; a mandatory supervision date of October, 1979; and a warrant-expiry date of June, 1981.

Although Roth had reached his full-parole eligibility date, he was applying only for day parole. He had been told by prison staff that, because of the serious nature of his offence, he would be wasting his time to apply for full parole.

Roth's victim was a forty-three-year-old nurse's aide named Mary Bowen who lived in a small house near the city transit line. Bowen had finished her shift at Calgary Hospital and had been home for about five minutes when Roth knocked on the door and asked if "Sharon" lived there. Bowen said no and Roth left. As a precaution, she locked the door and put on the security chain. At about 3 a.m. she was awakened by the sound of breaking glass. Terrified, she fled her bedroom to the kitchen to phone the police. Roth, who had now entered the dining-room by the broken window, seized her wrist as she was about to call. He forced her back to the bedroom and indecently assaulted her at knifepoint. This consisted of kissing and touching her breasts and private parts. The knife was an ordinary table knife owned by the victim. Roth then forced her to dress, warned her to keep quiet, and pulled her by the wrists out of the house. When he stumbled and fell on the unfamiliar pathway, Bowen ran off screaming for the house next door.

It had snowed earlier and the police were able to trace footsteps from Bowen's house to a nearby alley, where they found Roth hiding in an unlocked garage. He did not resist arrest, but later at the police station he went into "a sort of fit" and was placed in a straitjacket. He denied committing the offence, although he also claimed to remember nothing of his actions that night because he was "spaced right out" on alcohol and marijuana. (After the assault Bowen required psychiatric counselling. She sold her home and moved into a high-security residential complex.)

Attached to our file was a psychiatric assessment of Roth. It stated that the inmate believed that his mother was dead, and that he knew he had several brothers and sisters but had no idea where they were. He recalled that when he was about ten he had received a Christmas present from an older sister who he thought was called Lori but he had had no other contact with any family members. He had been told by one of his foster parents, when he was about thirteen, that one of his brothers had been shot, but he didn't know if this was true or any other details.

In the opinion of the psychiatrist, Roth's story that he was so "spaced out" that he didn't know what he was doing was probably true. The psychiatrist saw Roth less as a criminal than as a poorly socialized individual unable to handle his needs adequately. He believed Roth had little insight into why he behaved as he did, and without this understanding the psychiatrist thought he would likely re-offend. On the other hand, the professional pointed out, continued incarceration without treatment would likely reduce Roth's capacity to fit himself back into society eventually.

The prison staff member and the parole officer, known as the inmate's "team", differed in their recommendations. The prison staff member at that time was called a living unit development officer, or LUDO. The name has changed since then but the job function remains essentially the same — to work out a schedule of activities appropriate to each new inmate, and to be available to the inmate as an administrative liaison when problems arise. On the other hand the parole officer, or PO, works in the community and meets the inmate only when the inmate approaches parole eligibility date and requires an acceptable plan for his release to the community.

The LUDO said that Roth could not leave protective custody while he remained at "Drum" because he would be assaulted again, perhaps even more severely; word had gotten out that he was in on some kind of "skin" charge. Roth did not want to be transferred to another prison, as he feared that would delay his possible parole. (It takes several months before prison staff is willing to make an assessment on a new inmate.) Furthermore,

Roth valued his contact with AA's Ron Belan and considered him a valuable community support. The staff member concluded:

"I know Roth's not a strong case but the last thing this kid needs is to be warehoused without treatment. The AADAC program is excellent and Belan is willing to work closely with him. Right now he can't go to AA, can't get any counselling as there's a waiting-list of months, he can't do any upgrading and he's just going down. He's depressed and getting worse. I've spent a fair bit of time with him and he's highly motivated right now to do the AADAC program. He'll lose it if he's simply warehoused or transferred against his will."

The parole officer thought otherwise. His argument was simply that Roth was not ready to go out. He agreed that warehousing him was potentially destructive, but pointed out that it was Roth's own immaturity that had brought on the prison beating and his subsequent need for protective custody. He concluded:

"I talked to him just a couple of days ago and he's really a mess, weeping and feeling sorry for himself. He's nineteen going on fourteen. Not only does he have no insight into his own behaviour, he hasn't any job skills, doesn't have any friends or family support, has no social skills, and he has an addiction problem. He is extremely fragile, and if he goes out now I believe we'd be setting him up for failure."

A minute later Roth arrived, escorted by a guard. He looked young, gangling, nervous, and restless as he bounded across the room and slid into the chair placed in the middle of the desk opposite the board members. He reminded me of a frightened, pathetic animal caught in a trap. With a background like his, I thought, we'll have to handle him very gently to get anywhere near his core. My reveries were cut short by a roar from the board member who was to lead the case:

"Well, what have you got to say for yourself?" he barked,

slapping the desk with one hand while pushing his chair back from the table, distancing himself from the inmate. "Speak up, speak up!" he bellowed, "We can't hear you!"

My heart sank, my gorge rose. I was flooded with apprehension. God help me, what sort of a lunatic outfit had I joined? I looked at the others but their faces were as impassive as the Buddha's. I looked askance at Roth, who had sunk even further into his chair. After a long silence, in a voice quavering with fright, he said, "I'm applying for day parole."

"Day parole! Day parole!" roared the leading member, as if he had never heard of it before, as if Roth had invented the term. "You've got five years on a B&E and commit, and four years on forcible confinement and you're just lucky that those four years are concurrent and not consecutive. So just tell us, young fella, what you've been doing that would make us even dream of giving you a break! Speak up, speak up!"

Roth hesitantly offered that he was in PC so he hadn't been able to do much to show his progress towards rehabilitation. "I got beaten up a few weeks ago," he started to say, but my new colleague was already back in the fray.

"And whose fault was that?" he bellowed. "If you're dumb enough to get yourself into Drumheller in the first place and double-dumb enough to dislike natives you've no one but yourself to blame. Eh? Eh?"

"I'm not dumb," Roth said with surprising boldness, his acne-riddled chin jutting slightly forward with the words.

Hurrah! Good for you, Bobbie John, I wanted to shout. There's still some fight left in you. In spite of the repeated abandonments of your childhood and the degradation of your drunken adolescence you've managed to cling to some shreds of self-respect.

"You're not dumb? Not dumb?" the board member taunted him. "If you're not dumb, you're stupid. How come you're here if you're not dumb? You've got to be one or the other. So tell me, are you dumb or are you stupid?"

Today I find it difficult to believe that this outburst of contempt by the leading board member, an officially appointed representative of the government, actually happened. My notes confirm that it did, but I'll never know what these humiliating words did to Bobbie John Roth, to his fragile self-image, to his tattered self-esteem — the things he most needed to build on to lead a stable, law-abiding life. Fortunately, this was an isolated incident that I did not see repeated during my tenure on the board, although I was to witness other woefully misguided actions by other board members who, like this man, claimed to have only the best of intentions towards the inmates over whose fates they wielded such power.

The board voted to deny both day parole and full parole. While this decision was right in my judgement, the reasons for it disturbed me. I was profoundly shocked that after twenty months in prison this potentially salvageable young man whom everyone in the system recognized as needing some form of psychotherapy had received none. For fourteen months he'd mopped floors amid the general prison population and for six months he'd sat alone in a cage virtually all day. He had tried to help himself by attending AA, but AA was not set up to provide the broader treatment this angry, anti-social young man needed. Questioned briefly, Bobbie John revealed that he had no understanding of himself or his needs, no insight into why he hated natives, why he took drugs and alcohol, why he had assaulted his victim. He was the same person more or less as he had been when he entered prison.

In denying Roth's application, the board noted his need for some form of psychotherapy before his eventual release, and asked the prison psychologist to see him as soon as possible on a regular basis. If he reported progress in Roth's self-understanding, the board would consider a series of passes to AADAC's Recovery Acres before a possible day parole.

The prison psychologist met with the board the next day. He appeared harried, brushing his hair back with a nervous hand, ready to run. He already had a long waiting-list, he explained, and some of the men on it had been waiting for months and would probably be released before he could see them.

If he could see Roth, I asked, how long and how frequent would the sessions be? "Twenty minutes a client," he said, "and once or twice a month." He spoke with the breathless air of a man who, eight hours a day, day in and day out, tried to turn lives around in twenty-minute slots. "I just can't give them more than that. I try to get them reading, I've a supply of good books. Does Roth read?"

"With difficulty," the prison staff member replied.

"Oh Lord!" said the psychologist, and took off.

What I first took to be an unusual situation at Drum I later learned was the norm of prison life. Except for those who were severely disturbed such as pedophiles and rapists, who could be sent to one of Correctional Service's three regional psychiatric centres at Kingston, Saskatoon, or Matsqui, B.C., other inmates languished with perfunctory treatment or no treatment at all. With time I came to consider statements such as: "I am sentencing you to five years in prison where you will receive the psychiatric or psychological counselling that you require" to be among the most self-deluding words in the English language.

But this realization was to come only with the experience of going from one prison to another across the country. Meanwhile, I was here to learn the ropes from my more experienced peers. Finally, at about 4:30, when I was totally wiped out, the leading member turned to me and said: "Now you've heard enough. You know how to do it. You take the next case."

The final inmate of the day, one Rudolph Fricker, entered the room. An instantaneous current of vigorous dislike shot between us.

"Sit down, Mr. Fricker," I said to the short, plump man with reddish, thinning hair. I could not help noting that Fricker nodded to the male board members but ignored me completely.

I introduced my colleagues and said we understood that he was applying for a temporary absence program.

"That's right," he said, without so much as a glance my way. I ploughed ahead, going over briefly with him some of the facts that we had on file to ensure that all our information was correct.

Fricker had been born in Yugoslavia and had immigrated alone to Canada at the age of twenty following the death of his parents. He had worked in the Toronto area as a construction carpenter at first but later moved to Moncton, New Brunswick, where he finally opened his own cabinet-making shop. At thirty-eight, he married Christine Moore. It was her second marriage, his first. Mrs. Fricker had two children from her first union. Aged nine and seven, they attended a local school while she worked as a secretary in a Moncton office.

The marriage soon fell apart. One time the police were called because of a domestic fight during which Fricker smashed furniture. There was no police report of that incident but statements later made by a neighbour indicated that the living-room had been reduced to a shambles.

Soon after that the couple separated, and one month later Mrs. Fricker obtained a restraining order against Rudolph on the grounds that he was constantly harassing her, going to her new apartment, phoning her in the middle of the night, and turning up at her office uninvited and acting abusively. She told the police that she and both her children were frightened of him.

On the day of the offence, Fricker had put in ten hours of work at his shop. He was a hard and steady worker and since coming to Canada had managed to accumulate over $60,000 in savings, a small apartment that he rented out, and the home he and Mrs. Fricker had shared. After the separation, he had moved out of the house and rented it; at the time of the offence he was living with another couple, Rose and Ted Chernick.

Rose Chernick said that on the night of the offence she had cooked supper for her husband and Fricker, and that after she had washed up they all sat down to watch television. Fricker, who had just finished his third beer, suddenly stood up and said he was going downtown to buy cigarettes. Chernick said he would accompany him.

After purchasing the cigarettes, Fricker asked Chernick whether he would mind if they drove by his wife's residence. Chernick said okay. In a statement made later to police, Chernick said Fricker became more and more agitated as they approached his estranged wife's apartment building. Chernick told Fricker that he hoped that his friend wasn't going to do anything "foolish", as he wanted no part of it.

Fricker said that he just wanted to get a message to his wife about some mutual business, and asked that Chernick call Mrs. Fricker on the front-door intercom and ask her to come down. Chernick told Fricker to do it himself, but Fricker pointed out that the restraining order forbade him to go to his wife's residence.

Chernick obliged and a few minutes later Christine came downstairs. Staying inside, and with the lobby door opened only slightly, she asked Fricker what he wanted. Fricker said he had to talk to her about some of his tools that were missing. Christine said she had no tools whatsoever of his, told him to stop bothering her, and closed the door.

According to Chernick, Fricker returned to his truck and sat hunched over the wheel, breathing deeply and becoming progressively angrier. Chernick, now afraid, told Fricker he had to go home, at which point Fricker leaned across the cab and swung open the door. "Go home, then," he said. Chernick, unwilling to get into a fight, stepped out and waited on the pavement.

A car then drove up and parked a few feet in front of Fricker's truck. A middle-aged man got out, looked back at the truck, and went hurriedly into the building. Watching from below,

Fricker saw a light go on in his wife's living-room. The curtains were pulled aside slightly as Christine pointed out the truck to the man beside her. Fricker grabbed a 12-gauge shotgun from behind the seat, one of two guns that was in the truck, the other being a loaded .303 Savage. Chernick ran around to the driver's side just as Fricker jumped from the truck. He grabbed Fricker's sleeve, and Fricker turned the rifle on him. Then Fricker ran to the door and pushed all the intercom buttons. The door buzzed and Fricker shoved it open.

From upstairs, Mrs. Fricker and her friend, John Calvin Mitchell, forty-eight, an unmarried accountant with an excellent reputation in the Moncton community, had seen Fricker dash for the building and had heard their own buzzer sound. Within seconds there was pounding on the door. Mitchell told Mrs. Fricker to go and hide under the bed while he barricaded the door with a large mahogany sideboard.

Fricker blew out the locks, reloaded, and pushed against the door. Slowly the sideboard slid away. Edging the gun through the small opening, Fricker saw Mitchell. Deliberately he lowered the gun, aimed, and shot Mitchell in the chest, killing him instantly.

Neighbours called the police, who arrived within minutes. Mrs. Fricker was found in a state of shock in the bedroom. Her estranged husband was standing by Mitchell's body and readily acknowledged having shot him. Although he had never seen or met Mitchell before, he declared that the victim "deserved it for playing around with my wife behind my back".

Four months later Fricker was sentenced to three years on a charge of manslaughter. The Crown appealed the sentence and it was raised to five years. At the time of Fricker's parole board hearing, he had served twenty months and was eligible for parole. He had been seen by a psychiatrist, who could find no evidence of any psychiatric disorder.

My problems with this case didn't stop with Fricker's evident dislike for me and his general contempt for women. I was shocked that both his original sentence of three years and the final sentence of five years — with eligibility for parole after twenty months — were so short, in the light of his having killed an innocent man. I thought that if someone took a loaded gun with him wherever he went, and hung around his wife's home for weeks on end spying and stalking, the killing that followed should be designated not as manslaughter but as murder. Could it be that the courts held the view of a wife as chattel that was not dissimilar to Fricker's own attitude?

For now I cast these larger questions aside, content to accept the findings of the court and to concentrate on the immediate question of Fricker's parole application.

"Mr. Fricker," I said. "Do you know what it is that the board looks for when deciding whether to grant or deny parole?"

Fricker deigned to look at me. "Yeah, you want to know whether I'm going to do it again. Well, I'm not." He grinned heartily at my male colleagues.

"Mr. Fricker," I said, "we have three criteria for release and I would like you to completely understand them. It is *your* parole hearing, your chance to assure us that you meet them. The criteria are: first, whether you have gained what we call 'the maximum benefit' from incarceration; that is, have you learned all you can, changed as much as you can, from being incarcerated. Secondly, whether it would help your integration into society if you were released at this time. And thirdly — and in a case where there's violence this is our foremost consideration — whether you are or are not an undue danger to society, whether if you are frustrated or angered by someone you will do them physical harm."

"I've already told you I'm not going to do anything to anyone. What do you want me to say?" As he spoke he cocked his head to one side and narrowed his eyes, addressing everyone in the room but me. I thought it must have been extremely difficult for this older working-class European to cope with a woman in a position of authority.

"Tell us, Mr. Fricker, what you've learned about yourself since you've been here. You've been in prison twenty months and that's a long time to think over the actions that brought you here. Do you have any idea, for instance —"

"I don't remember anything," he interrupted loudly. "It's all in the files. I suppose you've read them?" He smirked at his own wit. "After I'd shoved the door open a bit I don't remember anything. The doctors explained it to me at the hospital . . . disassociation, that's what they call it. That's the state I was in when I did it," he finished triumphantly, dismissing any further discussion.

Clumsily I tried again. "Mr. Fricker, your prison supervision team has recommended a temporary absence program, but it's only a recommendation. It's up to the board to decide whether you will get a conditional release or not, and to make that decision we must be assured you are not a danger to the community."

"I've never done anything wrong, no record, this is my first offence," he said.

I seized on the point: "We know that, we know you normally led a law-abiding life. But there's another indication apart from the offence that you are capable of becoming uncontrollable when angry. Wasn't there an incident where you broke all the furniture in your living-room in a fit of anger?"

"So she told you that, did she, the bitch! Well, I never abused her. I wish I had! That's probably what she's hollering, that she's scared of me." He looked sullenly around the room.

I pointed out to Fricker that such statements only hurt his cause and that his time with the board would be better spent by giving us evidence of steps he had taken to gain some understanding and control of himself.

"Understanding of myself? Control of myself?" As he spoke his accent became stronger, his voice became strangled. It was as if I had pushed a button. "You know something, lady, I never stole, never. I earned my living since I was this high. We were successful, that damned woman and I, we worked hard at it. This was the first time in her life that she had any property possession. I built that house with my own hands on weekends, by myself. Nobody helped me, nobody's ever helped me."

Oh my God, I thought, he's going to cry.

"Okay," I said quickly, "so you've had a hard struggle all your life but you've always obeyed the law. What happened, Mr. Fricker?"

It took him a while to answer, then he said mournfully, "A life's a life. Had I realized what was going on it would never have happened. I feel terrible about it happening. Terrible. A life's a life. It wasn't the first time I went there. If I'd have known she was fooling around behind my back, no way would I have went there."

"Mr. Fricker!" I began. I was about to say his wife was not "fooling around" and it was not "behind his back", but to what end? He had successfully portrayed himself as the hard-working, simple-hearted peasant driven to a terrible act by jealousy. Nevertheless his tenacious persistence in laying claim to Christine Fricker in spite of a divorce in process, a restraining order, and his estranged wife's declared desire to be rid of him amounted to a dangerous obsession.

In its deliberations the board had to acknowledge the fact that Fricker had no previous offences, that he was, by conviction and habit, essentially a law-abiding, hard-working man. He had no major problem with alcohol nor with drugs and he had excellent supports in the community. All his friends had rallied around him and spoken of the offence as something totally "out of character". He had cared for his former wife's children extremely well, and there was no record or indication that he was ever abusive to them. Inside prison, although he did not have an alcohol problem, he had attended AA because it was the only self-help program available. He was also involved in various church activities. He had received good reports on his work as a cleaner. He was, in other words, perfectly capable of leading a useful, crime-free life.

On the negative side was the fact that he had gunned down an innocent man in a fit of murderous rage. He seemed unable to handle rejection or to accept the fact that his marriage to Christine was over, and there was nothing to indicate that this situation had changed.

The temporary absence (TA) program for which Fricker was applying would grant him a monthly forty-eight-hour pass to Calgary for a period of six months. One of the AA counsellors had volunteered to take Fricker shopping, or to a movie, and occasionally to have him home for a meal. The pass program would be for what was generally termed "socialization". Fricker had twenty more months to serve until his mandatory supervision date at which time, if he wasn't already out of prison, he had to be released by law.

"This guy isn't going to change," said the leading member, "even if he's left here for twenty years. The only question is whether he's going to go out and do something stupid, and I don't think there's any chance of that."

I tended reluctantly to agree. I had read in the community assessment report that Fricker's savings had been wiped out and that he had been forced to take a mortgage on his house to pay his lawyer. His criminal action had cost him his hard-earned life savings, and the likelihood of his repeating such an offence seemed to me negligible. A blustering, proud man, he had experienced prison as a profound humiliation, one that he would likely strive to avoid in the future.

"If we did give him the TA program," I said, "we could put some restrictions on it, for instance, that he's not to write or phone or make any contact whatsoever with his estranged wife. We could have him monitored closely. . . ." My voice trailed off. "I don't know . . . he just doesn't have enough control over his temper."

"Well, he doesn't have any charges inside," said the leading member in a surprising flash of sensitivity, "and if there's one place on earth that tests a fellow's temper it's being in this joint." He started tapping his fingers. "Come on, come on, we haven't all day. It's past six. We've been here since 8:30. Make up your mind."

I thought to myself, this is it. This is the crunch. I have to make a decision on someone else's life, in this cheaply furnished room at the end of nowhere with the snow blowing around outside and the windows rattling. The *only* way I can do it is by eliminating all considerations other than the prescribed criteria, because, frankly, I loathed Fricker.

Had Fricker received the maximum benefit from incarceration? Yes, he had learned a bitter lesson. His action had cost him dearly financially and psychologically. Beyond that he appeared quite incapable of learning. Would it assist his reintegration into the community if he were to obtain a release now? No doubt about it.

Finally, would his release constitute an "undue" danger to society? I had already looked up the precise meaning of "undue" in my dictionary: "exceeding what is appropriate or normal". So it would always be a judgement call and my judgement of Mr. Rudolph Fricker was that he was not an "undue" risk.

"I'm voting for a TA program," I said. "But only for twenty-four hours every month." Finally, after a bit of wrangling among the three of us, we reached an agreement. Fricker and the staff members were called back in.

"Mr. Fricker," I said, "we have decided to grant you a temporary absence program of twenty-four hours a month, starting in three months. If we receive any negative reports within that time the program will be cancelled. You will not be allowed to overnight anywhere except at a Calgary halfway house which will be designated. We are imposing three special conditions. First, that you make no attempt to contact in any way your former wife or stepchildren. Secondly, that you abstain from alcohol. You're not an alcoholic but alcohol is disinhibiting. Thirdly, that you do not have in your possession, on your person or available to you, a gun or any other weapon. If you fail to fulfill any of these conditions your program will be immediately cancelled. Do you understand these conditions?"

"Yeah. When do I get my day parole?" Fricker drawled contemptuously.

I could have picked up my briefcase and belted him on the head.

"This program starts in three months and runs for six," I said. "That will put you within eleven months of your mandatory supervision date. There will be plenty of time after we see how you do to discuss some sort of expansion of your release program."

Fricker stood up, shook hands with and thanked my male colleagues, turned and walked out of the room.

Back at the Hoo Doo Motel in Drumheller that night, I tried to prepare for the following day's cases, but my mind kept returning to Roth and Fricker. How was Roth doing now in his isolated cell, denied any release program? Wasn't there something intrinsically wrong with keeping Roth in and letting Fricker out? Roth's offence was vicious but he had not taken an innocent life. Did release on parole have little to do with the offence and nothing to do with justice? Did it have everything to do with all sorts of other extraneous, practical details, like community supports and survival skills and employability?

Fricker, who could have benefited from counselling, would have laughed at the idea. Roth, who desperately needed it, might get a little if he was lucky. So what were prisons for? Removal from society? But couldn't that be done without building isolated fortresses that cost millions of dollars to run? If punishment was supposed to fit the crime, shouldn't Roth have been given something by the board and shouldn't Fricker have been kept in?

I was beginning slowly to appreciate the multi-layered com-
plexities of the world I had entered, a world of many unspoken
rules and questions but few clear answers.

2   The Parole Process

Before we enter the shadow world of prisons and prisoners and start to weigh their crimes against their punishments, their rehabilitation against society's revenge, and before we look into the tangled knot of lust and love, of greed and generosity that is the human heart in both keeper and kept, we must first look at the physical organization of the National Parole Board, as well as at the procedures and policies under which its decisions regarding conditional liberation are made.

The National Parole Board is an independent administrative tribunal in the department of the ministry of the solicitor-general. The National Parole Service is under the authority of Correctional Service Canada (CSC): its officers act as information gatherers and supervisors of federal parolees released into the community by the parole board.

Offenders sentenced to less than two years are placed in provincial institutions. Quebec, British Columbia, and Ontario have provincial parole boards to deal with these inmates, but in the other provinces parole is the responsibility of the national board. There is an inequity here: provincial inmates in Quebec, British Columbia, and Ontario are personally interviewed by the provincial board, but in the other provinces, where cases are reviewed by the national board, the inmates are subject to a decision on paper.

When I arrived in Ottawa to join the National Parole Board in late January, 1978, Francis Fox was solicitor-general; before I left eight and a half years later six other solicitors-general had come and gone. There were only six board members who worked in Ottawa, and they padded around their offices on Laurier Street in what seemed to me — after a lifetime in ink-stained, paper-littered, noise-polluted city rooms — to be vast carpeted havens of silence and solemn cogitation. The other nineteen members were distributed among the board's five regional offices: Moncton (Atlantic region), Kingston (Ontario region), Montreal (Quebec region), Saskatoon (Prairies region), and Burnaby (Pacific region).

The Ottawa board members were not in the least homogeneous. This surprised me: I had expected them to be all of a kind with similar backgrounds, and some lively common interests and attitudes. Besides myself, there was a lawyer, an ex-chief of police, a part-time professor, an ex-deputy prison warden, a businessman, and a university psychologist. Our broad spectrum of attitudes and viewpoints often led to lively, if tensely polite, clashes when we met every morning in the boardroom for coffee. Overall we were a fusty and rather close-mouthed group. We seldom offered frank assessments of our own performances or revealed our prejudices. Used to the openness of west coast life, I found the circumspectness of Ottawa disorienting, and this impression did not change much during the years I spent there.

Ottawa members did not serve one particular region but worked wherever needed. For the first six years of my appointment I travelled for at least two weeks of every month, working in every minimum-, medium-, and maximum-security institution from Dorchester, near Moncton, New Brunswick, to Kent, near Agassiz, British Columbia. At busy times, such as the weeks before Christmas when the regional offices were swamped with requests from those eligible for temporary absence passes, we were on the road for six and seven weeks at a stretch.

As well as the twenty-five permanent (full-time) members,

there was a similar number of temporary (part-time) members. The latter were appointed through the same process as permanent members: essentially, friends in high political places submitted their names to Cabinet as possible appointees when vacancies occurred in their regions. In my own case, for instance, my name was initially submitted by Simma Holt, who was then a member of parliament for Vancouver-Kingsway. It was brought to Cabinet by Senator Ray Perrault of Vancouver, and supported by Prince Rupert's Iona Campagnolo, then minister of sports and fitness, and by Vancouver's Ron Basford, then minister of justice. All were aware of my deep interest in questions of social justice, in which I had done graduate studies.

Temporary members were brought in when full-time members could not handle the number of hearings that were requested by inmates and required by law. (There are now some eighty temporary members.) In addition to these, there were community members. The law required that two community members sit with regular members in parole hearings of inmates whose minimum sentences were life imprisonment, those condemned to death (before the abolition of the death penalty in 1976) whose sentences had been commuted to life, and those sentenced to an indeterminate period. Community members, like all board members, were appointed on a regional basis and, with few exceptions, they were men and women known for their community involvement. Some community member appointees — like some full-time or temporary members — were simply party hacks who were being paid off and had little interest in the work of the board. It did not take long for their real feelings to surface, however, and they were called upon to participate only when absolutely necessary.

In each region, and at headquarters, the chairman designated one member as the senior member. This person was responsible for his or her region's adherence to policy and for the smooth operation of the board in that area. Every couple of months the senior members met with the chairman in Ottawa as an executive committee to discuss and vote on various issues, primarily those of policy.

In reality, however, the executive committee often dealt more with the trappings of policy, or with the means of implementing policy that had already been decided by deputy ministers and senior bureaucrats working through and with the Justice Department, and the Secretariat of the Office of the Solicitor-General, and with the board's own senior staff.

How board policy was implemented in daily practice in hearings across the country can be best illustrated by a fictitious case history. I have chosen the case of "Doug Simms", which was drawn up by board staff as a teaching tool for use in police seminars and in the training of new board members, because it involved virtually every decision that the parole board is called upon to make.

In 1974 Doug Simms was sentenced to a seven-year term for two counts of rape. He had picked up two teenage female hitchhikers, driven them to a secluded spot, and raped them.

While in custody Simms sought counselling for his sexual problem. He applied several times to the parole board for a release program. In June, 1977, the board granted him day parole, a gradual form of release requiring him to return to either the institution or to a halfway house nightly.

By law, the board had to review Simms for full parole when he had served one-third of his sentence. The board could grant Simms a full parole if he met three criteria, criteria that apply to every release: 1) he had derived the maximum benefit from incarceration; 2) his reform and rehabilitation would be aided by the granting of parole; and 3) his release on parole would not constitute an undue risk to society.

The board did not grant Simms full parole at his 1977 review. Simms was scheduled to be released automatically, by law, in 1979 on mandatory supervision after having served two-thirds of his sentence. However, in a second review of his case in

March, 1978, the board decided that Simms met the three parole criteria and expanded his day parole to full parole. Simms agreed to abide by the following standard parole conditions, which apply to all parolees:

1. To remain until expiry of sentence in 1981 under the authority of the designated representative of the National Parole Board.

2. To proceed directly to the area designated in the instructions on release and, immediately upon arrival, to report to the parole supervisor (and to the police if this were made a condition of release).

3. To remain in the immediate designated area and not to leave that area without obtaining permission beforehand from the parole board representative through the parole supervisor.

4. To endeavour to maintain steady employment and to report at once to the parole supervisor any change or termination of employment or any other change of circumstances such as accident or illness.

5. To obtain approval from the representative of the National Parole Board, through the parole supervisor before a) purchasing of motor vehicle; b) incurring debts by borrowing money or instalment buying; c) assuming additional responsibilities such as marrying; d) owning or carrying firearms or other weapons.

6. To communicate immediately with the parole supervisor or the representative of the parole board if arrested or questioned by police regarding any offence.

7. To obey the law and fulfill all legal and social responsibilities.

Once released, Simms was supervised on behalf of the National Parole Board by a parole officer employed by Correctional Service Canada. The parole board delegated to CSC the authority to suspend Simms's parole and have him returned to custody if necessary and desirable to do so in the event of a breach of any term or condition of parole or to prevent a breach of any term or condition of parole or to protect society.

The parole officer suspended Simms's parole on May 3, 1979 for reasons contained in a report which follows. The officer had fourteen days from the date that Simms was suspended to decide either to cancel the suspension and reinstate Simms's parole, or to recommend that the board revoke his parole. In such a case his sentence would be recalculated and he would not be released automatically on mandatory supervision until January, 1980.

In the original of this training document, a lengthy parole supervisor's report follows. It includes a report on where Simms was employed (at a dry cleaners), how he spent his leisure time (with his wife and her two children), his response towards supervision (weekly contact, co-operative), and the reason for the suspension. We will deal only with the section on reasons for suspension because it directly relates to the decisions that were made and the procedures that were followed.

The parole officer's report stated:

> On or about May 3, 1979, Simms was arrested by the Winnipeg police and charged with unlawful confine-ment. Suspension warrants were prepared on May 3 and Simms was taken to Stony Mountain Institution, the prison from which he previously had been released.
>
> Simms appeared at a preliminary hearing, pleaded not guilty and the trial date was set for August 14, 1979.
>
> The circumstances of offence for which he was charged are as follows: On Tuesday, May 1, 1979, between noon and 1:00 p.m. a fifteen-year-old female hitchhiker was picked up on the northern outskirts of Winnipeg and taken to a destination in St. Boniface. On the way, the driver told the hitchhiker he wanted to drop

off some papers before he headed for his destination. Instead, he took her to St. Boniface Park, where an attempt was made to keep her in the car. She managed to fight him off, fell out of the car, and took off into the bushes. The driver managed to talk her into returning to the car when he apologized, telling her that he thought she was a different type of girl and that he did not intend to hurt her.

She agreed to sit in the back seat after being assured he intended to drive slowly so she could jump out if she felt he meant her any harm. He then drove her to Main Street, where he let her out.

The preliminary police enquiries to this point included a description of the vehicle and the driver whose description resembled Simms.

The parole officer's report continued:

I contacted Simms at his place of work and informed him that the police wished to have him participate in a line-up. He agreed to co-operate fully and the officers drove to his place of work.

I decided at this point to prepare suspension warrants in the event Simms was picked out of the line-up. This decision was based on my concern that the circumstances surrounding this incident were similar to the *modus operandi* of the rape offences for which he was originally convicted.

The police informed me that Simms was picked out of the line-up by the female hitchhiker without any hesitation. A charge of unlawful confinement was under consideration to be reviewed with the Crown counsel next morning.

The following day the parole officer interviewed Simms at the Winnipeg police station following his court appearance. In this interview Simms broke down and cried, swearing at his own stupidity in picking up a hitchhiker. He said he initially thought the hitchhiker was a boy and was surprised when she turned out to be a girl. In any case, he decided to continue his trip to St. Boniface Park and when he got there, he reached for his coat on the back seat, and, he said, "The girl went bananas." She panicked further when he grabbed her by the wrists and tried to calm her down. He begged her not to freak out on him but she got out of the car while he was still holding one of her wrists. He let go to assure her he meant no harm. He said he felt badly about letting her walk and drove up to her and convinced her to get into the back seat. He then drove to Main Street and dropped her off. Simms swore he had absolutely no intention of hurting her.

He maintained he had done a stupid thing and bemoaned the fact that his actions had hurt his wife and children. He denied ever picking up other hitchhikers except in the company of his wife, when they picked up only males. He knew it was risky to pick up female hitchhikers, especially when he was alone.

Nine days later the parole officer again interviewed Simms, who by then was back in prison. Simms guardedly wondered aloud if he had picked up the girl just to prove to himself and to "the world" that he could feel comfortable being alone with a female other than his wife. He said that since his release on day parole he was always fearful about being alone with another woman.

When the parole officer tried to make sure he fully understood why he had been suspended and why he was going to recommend to the board that Simms's parole be revoked, Simms became hostile and defensive, saying repeatedly, "But I did not rape the girl." He then asked the parole officer to help him get a transfer to the Regional Psychiatric Centre (RPC) in Saskatoon, where he could get help in understanding the reasons for his actions.

The parole officer decided to refer the case to the board with the recommendation that Simms's parole be revoked. He reasoned that Simms was not doing as well as expected even though he had a job, a devoted wife, loving children, community support, and professional psychological help available whenever he needed it. Ultimately, the parole officer did not feel he could ignore the similarity between this incident and Simms's past behaviour.

As soon as Simms's case was referred to the board for a decision, he had the right to apply for and receive a post-suspension hearing with the board. Simms applied for and received a hearing on June 7, 1979, four and a half weeks after his suspension. (The board is required to give a suspended person fourteen days' advance notice of the date of hearing.)

Present at that hearing were Simms, two board members, the parole officer, an institutional caseworker, and an assistant. The assistant is invited by the inmate and must be security-cleared by the institution. He or she can be a wife, family member, friend, pastor, lawyer, employer, fellow worker, virtually anyone. Simms chose to have his lawyer.

The decision to be made by the board was either to cancel the suspension or to revoke the parole. The members who decide the case must agree; if they cannot it must be heard again by other members.

After one of the board members had stated all the information the board had relating to the revocation, Simms asked the board if it would postpone its decision until the court had disposed of the unlawful confinement charge. It is worth noting here that the board had received numerous letters of support from Simms's employer and friends, and that Simms's lawyer believed that the Crown's case was weak. The board members said that the disposition of the case was not part of the board's duty and pointed out that its decision must be based on Simms's performance up to the date of the suspension.

Simms then said he had no intention of hurting the girl, which was also the argument of his community supporters. He said that he did not realize the hitchhiker was a girl until he stopped and would have "felt like an ass if I drove away". He recalled that he had been concerned when he recognized her sex, but felt he could handle the situation and agreed to drive her to St. Boniface, her stated destination.

He said he drove to St. Boniface Park, which was a very public place, and that he did not rape her, attack her, or hurt her. "When she went bananas," he said, "it scared the hell out of me. All I did was reach into the back seat for my jacket and she reacted. I told her there was no reason for panic and then I drove her back to the city."

At this point Simms's assistant had his turn. Assistants are allowed to advise the suspended person on any question and have ten minutes at the end of the hearing to present additional information to the board. The lawyer said a) that Simms should be considered innocent until proven guilty by the courts; b) that he did not breach any of the conditions of his parole; and c) that his parole should be reinstated immediately if the board had no evidence that he was an undue risk to society.

The board members then asked everyone to leave the hearing-room while they discussed the case and made their decision. After a brief discussion, they decided that Simms's parole should be revoked. They wrote the following reasons for this decision and these were read to Simms when he and his assistant returned.

> When Simms was seen at the post-suspension hearing there were strong positives and strong negatives. The pattern of his behaviour is the same as in his previous sexual assaults. To Simms's credit is the fact that he did not carry through.
>
> Whether the court finds him guilty or not is not pertinent at this time. It is our job to decide whether he is a risk or not to members of the community. The behaviour associated with the incident is far too similar to that

of previous assaults and shows a weakness in his personal controls discipline, a weakness which makes him
an undue risk.

It is our conclusion that he is a risk and for this reason
we have decided on revocation with a further review to
take place after he has undergone further counselling
and/or therapy. One year for the review would be
appropriate.

As well as informing Simms orally of the decision and its
reasons for it, the board was required to write to Simms stating
those reasons within fifteen days of revoking his parole. The
board's June 30, 1979, letter to Simms contained the following:

The board has concluded that the recent incident resulting in your arrest did demonstrate a loss of judgement
and personal controls. This in our opinion poses an
undue risk to the community. The board strongly rec-
ommends further counselling and therapy, so that you
might gain from this experience and not lose the excellent progress you have made over the last few years.

The letter also explained to Simms that he had the right to
have this decision re-examined by other board members who
had not participated in the revocation decision. Simms applied
for the re-examination. His appeal was handled by a group of
three board members based in Ottawa called the internal review
committee, later renamed the appeal division. This committee
reviews cases but does not interview the inmate.

The internal review committee had the power to overturn the
previous decision if one or more of the following conditions
applied: a) the reasons given for a decision did not support the
decision; b) there was significant information in existence at the
time of review which was not considered; c) there was an error
in fact or in law; or d) there was new evidence not available at
the time of the earlier review. The committee would then

review — not in committee but individually — the entire file, including all recent reports as well as the board members' reasons for the decision they had taken.

Then the committee could either: a) affirm the board's decision and let the revocation stand; b) overturn the previous decision and cancel the revocation (Simms would then resume his parole); or c) order another hearing for Simms, because of new information or information that should have been considered but was not.

Simms decided to request that the decision to revoke his parole be re-examined on the following grounds:

1. "There is significant information which will arise from my trial on the charge which led to my suspension";

2. "The reasons for the revocation should be reconsidered . . . in view of the fact that the board did nót have any judicial assessment of the facts of the case nor even a transcript of the evidence before it when reaching its decision";

3. "Had the facts been reviewed on the basis of the above documents, rather than on a limited police report, the board might have come to a different conclusion and might have considered a return to day parole status or some less all-inclusive decision."

Simms then asked the appeal committee whether the board would be willing to reconsider its decision "in the event of an acquittal on the charge from this incident".

After studying the case the committee found no grounds on which to overturn the original decision and sent Simms the following letter:

> The evidence at hand indicates that the board acted properly in revoking your parole. We recognize the gains that you have made and encourage you to continue the kind of treatment that has obviously led to improved self-management. At the same time, the incident and the significance of the incident, in the context of your past

criminal acts and the threat to society implicit in such acts, cannot be ignored. The data that may arise from the trial cannot be taken into consideration at this time nor can they be used to implement a lesser form of release at this time.

With this final decision, Simms's mandatory supervision date was recalculated and he was scheduled for release in January, 1980. His release would be automatic by law and he would be subject to the same seven parole conditions stated earlier.

The board will have only one more decision to make regarding Simms. Several weeks before his release date Correctional Service Canada will provide a report assessing his progress, attitude, activities, and general status. The board will then decide whether or not it would be appropriate to add a special condition to Simms's mandatory supervision certificate. If it decides that a special condition, such as "To abstain from alcohol", is appropriate, this will be typed onto the certificate.

These are the main processes within which real and imperfect people have to make decisions about other real and imperfect people. Such is the skeletal framework within which the board exercises its mandate.

3   *A Duty To Act Fairly*

Men and women who are sentenced to a term in the penitentiary, kept under lock and key away from the public whose laws they have broken, are not generally regarded as persons of significant worth. It is not surprising that those who deal with them, mainly prison staff and occasionally parole boards, have developed relatively authoritarian and biased ways of treating them. Many of these attitudes are based on a stereotyped evaluation of an inmate's inability to handle his or her own life.

Fair treatment of inmates is as much an economic issue as a humanitarian one, because unfair treatment greatly reduces the chance of an inmate's rehabilitation. All inmates — even those sentenced to "life" imprisonment — sooner or later return to live in the community with the rest of us, so fair treatment is greatly in society's interest.

This realization is not new. In 1879, Inspector Moylan, then Inspector of Penitentiaries at Kingston, set forth a series of principles and propositions designed to curtail the abuse of power and to ensure fairness within prison walls. He wrote:

> It is of paramount necessity that prisoners should realize the fact that the rules are carried out fairly and justly, in order that strict and stern discipline be maintained without exciting constant resistance. They must feel, too, that the officers are simply administering the law, and that in

any case of abuse of power on the part of an officer, he will be held to a strict accountability.

Experience shows that there is no greater mistake in the whole compass of prison discipline than the studied imposition of personal degradation as part and parcel of the punishment.

More than a century has elapsed since these words were written, which indicates how slowly we learn when it comes to dealing effectively with those who have committed offences against society, and how slowly things change behind prison walls.

The basic principle of "fairness" and the universal resentment of "unfair" treatment are understood by everyone. Yet it has taken the determined efforts of scores of various individuals, not least among them dedicated lawyers and feisty prisoners, over the last fifteen years to rouse the Canadian justice system to an awareness of the need for fairer treatment of inmates. Eventually their efforts have been supported in law by the Canadian Human Rights Act of 1977; the Charter of Rights and Freedoms, 1981; the Privacy Act, 1982 (which supplemented and reinforced provisions concerning privacy in the Canadian Human Rights Act); and the Access to Information Act, which took effect in 1983.

During my term on the National Parole Board, we members gradually became aware that questions of fairness were not being given adequate attention in the course of parole hearings, and that new clearly defined procedures and rules for parole board hearings had to be developed and applied to ensure that inmates received fair treatment in the course of these hearings. At the time I joined the board, policy required that reasons be given for every negative decision made. In previous years this had not been the case. Inmates had been simply told yes or no, and never a reason for the answer. According to some old-time board members, inmates were as often as not given "a good tongue lashing" to boot.

Nobody, not even Parliament, had the right to demand that the board explain its decisions, decisions that were taken behind closed doors in secret by persons unknown to the public. This secrecy didn't seem to bother anybody — except on those rare occasions when a case went "bad"; then the secrecy of the board was perceived as a measure of its incompetence.

By 1978, as well as giving reasons orally for their decisions, board members also wrote comments to explain further the reasons for the way they had voted. These comments were written immediately after the conclusion of each hearing and were intended not only to clarify reasons for the vote, but also to note other particulars of the hearing, the general atmosphere, and any specific suggestions or instructions that the board might have given the inmate, such as that it would consider another parole application only after the inmate had involved himself in a drug/alcohol addiction program. During this time in the board's history, not every member who voted on a case attended its hearing. For instance, in cases that required seven votes, such as life sentences, only three members would attend the hearing, the other four making a "paper decision" on the case at the office. In such instances the written comments of members who had attended the hearing informed the absent member about what took place.

These comments were not shown to the inmate, but the decision and the reasons for it were either shared with the inmate immediately following the hearing or sent by letter to him or her as soon as the office voting was complete. The inmate could then ask that any negative decision, other than one concerning an unescorted temporary absence, be reviewed by the internal review committee, now known as the appeal division, which could reverse the original decision or order a new hearing.

The greatest impact on the National Parole Board of the landmark human rights legislation that marked the years of 1974–1984 centred on the question of "fairness", in particular on the manner in which board members conducted hearings. Before I deal with this, it is necessary to explain who attended hearings and what their role was. I should point out that the personnel who attend the hearings today remain the same as in 1978, except for the addition of an inmate "assistant", whose role is discussed in Chapter 5.

At least five people attended each hearing: the inmate, two or three board members (the number depended on length of sentence), a parole officer (PO), a living unit development officer (LUDO), and sometimes a prison psychologist, teacher, or staff member from a self-help group.

The parole officer and the living unit development officer were seldom neutral about a case. With the exception of a few who were lazy or rigid, these staff members were an experienced and thoughtful group, efficient and good-humoured in an atmosphere that simmered with pressure, frustration, covert violence, and overt nuttiness. In that bitter and angry world, a small army of dedicated yuppie-aged men and women existed who cared little about the consumer trappings of a successful life. Their idea of success was having one of "their" inmates "make it" on the street. Nor did they define inmates by their sentences or by their status as prisoners; rather they saw them as human beings caught up in messes of their own making and struggling to get out. It took a lot of integrity and vision to hang onto an attitude like that in the face not only of public dislike of inmates, but of the immaturity and self-centredness of many inmates themselves.

The LUDO's task at the hearing was to give an assessment of the inmate's attitude and performance on the "inside" and to recommend a grant or denial of parole. Details of the inmate's institutional life were included in this report — whether or not he was going to school (if there were any school); if, and where, he was working (if any work were available); whether he was in any life-skills classes (if there were any life-skills classes), or Toastmasters meetings (if any), or Alcoholics Anonymous groups (if any).

There was information about the inmate's health, personal habits, who he associated with, and whether he had any visitors. In sum, anything that would assist the board members in understanding what changes, if any, had occurred since the day the inmate had arrived at the prison, been searched, photographed, and numbered.

The PO, usually the same person who would be the inmate's supervisor on the outside, was there to describe any outside supports that would be available if the inmate were released. The PO would have interviewed the inmate and personally checked out his community supports. If the inmate had applied for day parole, the availability of a bed in a suitable halfway house would be confirmed. If the inmate had given the name of a prospective employer, the PO would have spoken to the employer to confirm that a job did exist and what it was. The PO would also visit the inmate's family, if he had one, and report on home conditions, employment of family members, and their overall attitude.

Both the LUDO's and PO's reports, assessments, and recommendations would be sent to the parole board's regional office prior to the hearing and would be part of the inmate's file. A résumé of three or four pages — longer if psychiatric or psychological reports were included — was prepared on each case by board staff to assist members. Even so, the workload was often so heavy that members arrived at their hotels looking like packhorses, hauling bulging cases of files to be studied overnight.

Having the PO and LUDO attend the hearings in person gave board members a chance to question them on their recommendations, and to be brought up to date on any changes in an inmate's status. For instance, between the writing of the

LUDO's or PO's report and the holding of the hearing, the inmate might have committed an institutional disciplinary offence, under Section 39 of the Penitentiary Service Regulations. While some of these offences could be quite serious, others are so ill-defined by the regulations as to allow for, if not invite, arbitrary reaction on the part of those in control. Unless the offence was a proven and serious one, such as an attempted escape or a physical assault or something that clearly indicated that the inmate was a bad parole risk, I felt it unfair to give the charge much weight in the hearing, as the inmate had already been punished by a loss of a day or two of remission, a few nights of lockup, and loss of recreation activities, or even a few days in the "hole" or "digger" (solitary confinement). For inmates who had been locked up for years, "sounding off" at a guard or an official when under duress sometimes seemed to me more a positive than a negative action, for it indicated that years of institutionalized living had not shattered their spirit.

Also, by attending the hearing the prison staff could see how the inmate handled himself under the pressure of that situation, which could foreshadow how the inmate might cope with the stress of the street after being made as dependent as a child for years.

When all of us were settled in for a hearing, it was customary to discuss the case we were about to hear before the inmate arrived. Talk was casual but to the point: "He's a tough one, but the women love him," a LUDO might say. "Three different women visit him and none of them knows about the other two." Or: "I've never known anyone to be as manipulative as that guy. He really knows how to keep the pressure up to get what he wants." Or a PO might say: "We talked for quite a while, but I never felt I really made contact with him, almost as if he wasn't coming straight."

Staff would talk about the prisoner's correspondence, phone calls, visitors. "Joe came back to his range looking really down on Sunday. His wife visited and I think they had a row," a staffer might say. A board member would ask: "What do you think it was about?" The staffer might shrug: "I've heard his name mentioned in connection with drugs. Maybe he asked her to pack for him and she refused." The board members would be unable to forget this speculation during their deliberations, even though there was not a shred of evidence to support it. Once told something negative about an inmate, even a suspicion, I had to make a deliberate effort to wipe my mind clear of it when weighing the pros and cons of a release. Sometimes the rumour was of such a grave nature — for instance, suspicion of involvement in a stabbing or of trafficking in drugs — that it could not be cavalierly discounted in deciding whether or not an inmate posed any threat to the community.

The first few times this happened I was surprised and uncomfortable. This sort of exchange was much like gossip, which I dislike. After a while, however, I grew used to it. Who was I to look down on an established practice that did not seem to bother anyone else? The parole board was under the solicitor-general's department and I blithely assumed it would not act in any way that was not just and legal. By the time I'd been on the board a year I'd been co-opted by the system: any scruples I had entertained had faded and the pre-hearing rap sessions seemed to be not only an essential part of the hearing, but sometimes also the actual crux of the hearing.

It was also during these pre-hearing rap sessions that we would be given factual information that had been gained by surreptitious means, such as tapping the inmate's phone calls (inmates are allowed a certain number of phone calls monthly, depending on the security rating of the institution), opening the inmate's mail, or by another inmate ratting on someone or sending out a "kite" (unsigned letter). Or sometimes an inmate's spouse or girlfriend would write in confidence to the institution or the board, expressing concern regarding the inmate's release. The inmate would not be told that the board had received this information, and so would not know that part of the case against him and would have no opportunity to explain, deny, or defend his actions. When this "confidential information" resulted in a denial of parole, the inmate would be told that he had "not received the maximum benefit of incarceration", or some such mumbo-jumbo.

I now believe strongly that at the time I joined the board inmates were treated (both by the penitentiary staff and by the parole board) with a lack of fairness that would not have been tolerated anywhere else in society. These practices were simply the result of inmates being regarded as second-class citizens not entitled to the standards of natural justice and fair play with which ordinary citizens could expect to be treated. Inmates were considered in some respects to be hostages of arbitrary fortune, deservedly so because they had been found guilty and sentenced in a court of law. The extent to which an individual inmate received treatment that he could be expected to think of as fair — in comparison with the treatment of other inmates — depended to a considerable extent on the whims of individual parole board members and of correctional service staff members. That the treatment of individuals was sometimes arbitrary and unequal between individual inmates only became apparent to me as I began to think of them as individuals, and not just as members of a group requiring control and discipline.

Sometimes we would turn up for a hearing only to find that an inmate on our hearing-list had just been transferred to another prison in another province. Or that several parole applicants had "disappeared" in the same way. Transferring men across the country — often taking them from their cells in the middle of the night — was a common way for a warden to keep the lid on his prison. Or he would shift them around just to "stir them up", to reduce the danger of the inmates organizing. The move would mean the inmate's hearing, to which he was entitled by law, would be arbitrarily postponed, and his chances of parole were automatically reduced, because it takes an inmate several weeks to settle into a new situation and prison staff members several months before they feel they have sufficient knowledge of him to give a recommendation on parole.

The fact that an inmate's family was located in the same city — having already moved the household to be near him — was not considered in these transfers, nor was a wife's financial inability to follow her husband to the new institution.

After the assistant system was introduced, when we had to strike an inmate off our list because of his transfer, we would sometimes learn during our hearings that a wife or a parent, not advised of the transfer, had been turned away at the prison door. Many of these assistants were poor, and most prisons are remote. I found most painful the thought of the long, ill-afforded journey ending with a shut door and the statement that they would be advised of the transfer by mail. These people were not inmates but in their own way they, too, were victims of the system.

At first, I saw many of the penitentiary system's disciplinary rules as paranoid or just silly, but with time I learned that there was a reason for most of them, for example, a pillow fight in a dormitory for young men can be used as a cover for a stabbing or gang rape. But I never got used to the capriciousness of the range of punishments. In one medium-security institution "disrespectful" language to a guard was regarded as a minor breach worth two nights' lockup and loss of recreation; in another it was regarded as a major infraction that resulted in seven days in solitary confinement and seven days' lost remission. Inmates resented the arbitrariness of the discretionary action a guard could take, and the equal arbitrariness of the penalties that would result, and often in hearings they aired their feelings of being treated "unfairly".

The contribution to unfair treatment that is made by the size and atmosphere of prisons is another reality too powerful to dismiss. Prisons are usually massive buildings that consume one's range of vision and fill the mind with their image of impregnability. Inside, past the mass of heavy stone, a paramilitary ambience prevails. There are the uniforms, the bars, the electronic doors, the slam of the door bolt like a shot from a gun, the guards watching unseen behind plates of black glass. The guards, the other staff members, and the parole board members come and go freely. But the "others" must stay behind the second interior wall. It is hard not to fall prey to seeing the split as a primeval struggle between good and evil. Being intelligent, educated, and compassionate does not guarantee that a prison staffer or board member will be fair. It is possible to be all these things and still be blinded by one's own ego. When "we" were required to make a judgement about "them", there was a strong tendency — unless one had a great deal of professional experience or training in some related area prior to being appointed to the board — to become paternalistic, to adopt an attitude of "We know what's best for you", or "We have to be cruel to be kind", or "Trust us, for we are wise and good."

In the red-carpeted chambers of various courts across the land, however, forces were stirring that would change the attitudes of many of those who worked in the corrections field. The movement to bring the penitentiaries, the parole board, and the police into the twenty-first century was under way. We were about to be forced by prisoners' rights advocates to adopt fairness as a key principle, and this would dramatically reform the system.

I am not a lawyer, and these constitutional challenges will no doubt be the subject of books written by those competent to do so. I will mention in passing only five of the many cases that effected change in the board's functioning. I will then deal in detail with two other significant cases — *Mason and the Queen*, and *Wayne William O'Brien v. National Parole Board* — for in these two cases not only were some of the issues in the other five cases considered judicially, but more important in the consideration of the legal issues involved and in the judgements rendered, Ontario High Court Justice Ewaschuk and Federal Court Justice McNair also illuminated the spirit of the law and the direction that the National Parole Board was obliged to take.

The first case that heralded substantial change was that of *Martineau v. Matsqui Institutional Disciplinary Board*. It started in 1976 — a year before the Canadian Human Rights Act was passed — when a legal colleague asked John Conroy, another lawyer, to represent his client in a prison disciplinary hearing. Conroy agreed, called Matsqui prison, and asked when the hearing would be. He was told in so many words: "You can't come here! It's a prison! You can't represent an inmate at a disciplinary court!"

Conroy wondered why not. His client, Robert "Chico" Martineau, had not been told the case against him, so he had no chance of responding to the charges. "Once an inmate goes to prison does he lose *all* his rights? Can a prison discipline an inmate as it likes without accountability to anyone? Who gave the warden this right, and who gave the prison disciplinary committee its powers?" Conroy asked.

He decided to take the case to court but this proved to be no easy matter. Nobody seemed sure what court he should go to. Was a prison disciplinary hearing purely administrative; was it quasi-judicial or judicial? In the end Conroy started two actions, one in Federal Court Trial Division and one in the Federal Court of Appeal. The Federal Court of Appeal ruled that the disciplinary commissioner's directives did not have the force of law, and therefore the disciplinary hearing was a tribunal. This was challenged, but the Supreme Court of Canada agreed with the Appeal Court.

The issue went to the Supreme Court twice and after four years that court came out with a major ruling in 1980, in which Mr. Justice Brian Dickson stated: "The [disciplinary] board's decision had the effect of depriving an individual of his liberty by committing him to a 'prison within a prison'. In these circumstances, elementary justice requires some procedural protection. The rule of law must run within penitentiary walls."

This finding served notice on the parole board that its regulations, policy, procedures, and processes would soon fall under close examination. Board policy could be changed by the executive committee of the board (composed of senior staff members and the senior board member in each region) but regulations had to be approved by the Governor-in-Council (the Cabinet) and the process was often paralyzingly slow.

On December 2, 1981, the Charter of Rights and Freedoms, which found it "desirable to provide in the Constitution of Canada for the recognition of certain fundamental rights and freedoms" was passed by the House of Commons and was immediately approved by the Senate.

In June, 1982, following a suit filed by Toronto lawyer David Cole, *Couperthwaite v. National Parole Board* the Supreme Court ruled that there could be no discussion of a case without the inmate being present, for if he were absent when any part of his case were being discussed he could be left without access to information that had some influence on the board's decision. It was decided that this lack of access to all information would offend against procedural fairness.

At the same time as this judgment, new ground was broken by Mr. Justice Potts on his ruling in *R. v. Cadeddu* by holding that section 7 of the Charter requires that a parolee be given the opportunity for an in-person hearing before his parole can be revoked.

Rulings on two more cases, *Dubeau* and *Morgan*, quickly followed. Both these inmates had asked that lawyers be present at their hearings. The parole board had refused them the right, only to be instructed by the court that inmates were entitled to an assistant and that assistant could be a lawyer as long as she or he acted as a friend and not as a lawyer.

The case of *Mason and the Queen* was argued before Mr. Justice Ewaschuk of the Ontario High Court. An application for habeas corpus was made by P.M. Zylberberg on behalf of Mason, with C.P. Kobernick, for the respondent, the Attorney-

General of Canada. The issue to be determined was the legality of detaining Mason after the parole board had revoked his mandatory supervision. Mason had been released from Collins Bay Penitentiary, near Kingston, Ontario, on mandatory supervision on March 6, 1983. His MS was due to expire on April 27, 1984, when he reached his warrant expiry date. On March 18, 1983, Mason was convicted of new offences and his mandatory supervision was suspended, then revoked by a vote of board members, and Mason was re-incarcerated. He then requested a post-revocation hearing, which was held on April 14, 1983.

In his judgment given on September 15, 1983, Mr. Justice Ewaschuk described the post-revocation hearing and the procedures that followed.

"Two members of the National Parole Board attended at the hearing wherein the applicant was present and made submissions with the assistance of a personal friend. He elected not to have legal counsel. Unfortunately, the two members of the Board disagreed — one deciding that mandatory supervision should be continued; the other that it should be revoked."

Section 24(2)(b)of the Parole Regulations provided that a third vote be cast in such cases.

"However," said Mr. Justice Ewaschuk, "the deciding vote was not cast by a person who was present at the hearing. As a result, that board member did not hear the evidence of the prisoner and his assistant's submissions. Thus . . . an absentee member of the board, presumably stationed in Ottawa, decided to cancel the applicant's liberty in Sudbury, his place of detention. Since that time, the inmate has been transferred to Collins Bay Penitentiary."

The applicant's basic complaint, said the judge, was that he had been deprived of his liberty in a fundamentally unjust manner, and that Section 24(2)(b) of the Parole Regulations, by allowing an absentee third vote, violated Section 7 of the Canadian Charter of Rights and Freedoms, which guaranteed procedural due process, that is, natural justice. Mr. Justice Ewaschuk also referred to Section 20.1(3) of the Parole Regulations, which provided that an assistant be present at the hearing and address board members at the conclusion of the hearing.

In this case, said Mr. Justice Ewaschuk, "the critical third board member did not see the inmate nor his assistant, nor did he hear their submissions in person. Instead, he became a faceless and absent bureaucrat who cast his critical vote in some distant unknown place. And as important, the third member perforce decided against liberty on the basis of written materials and not a personal plea."

Mr. Justice Ewaschuk found that this was not the "fair and decent procedure" required by the "fundamental justice" provision of Section 7 of the Charter and that the procedures allowed for in Section 24(2)(b) of the Parole Regulations were inherently unfair. Stating that an inmate must be afforded an in-person hearing before each board member necessary to constitute a full panel in each particular case, he ordered a new hearing for Mason before three board members who had not heard the case previously. The hearing was held, and Mason's mandatory supervision was again revoked.

The question of whether "he who decides must also be he who hears [the case]" was also at the heart of the next case, *Wayne William O'Brien v. National Parole Board*. A Toronto lawyer, David P. Cole, appeared for O'Brien and J. A. Pethes for the Attorney-General of Canada.

O'Brien, who was serving a life sentence for second-degree murder, had been denied an unescorted temporary absence in a seven-member vote for which only three members attended the hearing. O'Brien charged procedural unfairness under Section 7 of the Charter because not all those voting on his case saw or heard his submission in person.

In his lengthy judgment on November 23, 1984, Mr. Justice McNair of the Federal Court Trial Division noted that the parole board was not legally obliged to hold a hearing on O'Brien's application for an unescorted temporary absence but had held one nonetheless.

"In my opinion," said Mr. Justice McNair, "what the case essentially comes down to is simply this: once having extended the latitude of fair review procedure and embarked on a hearing, does the duty of fairness then dictate that all members of the board required to vote must have personally seen and heard the applicant before casting the final ballot?" He went on to say that even though it was a voluntary hearing there should be a proper balance between administrative practicability and the minimum requirements of fairness, and "room must always be left for the implication of an impression of justice appearing to be done."

Mr. Justice McNair also looked to the *Martineau* case and quoted the test formulated by Mr. Justice Dickson: "'In the final analysis, the simple question to be answered is this: Did the tribunal on the facts of the particular case act fairly towards the person claiming to be aggrieved? It seems to me that this is the underlying question which the courts have sought to answer in all cases dealing with natural justice and fairness.'"

Applying this test, Mr. Justice McNair found that the board did not act fairly towards O'Brien, who should have been given an in-person hearing before all members of the board who voted on his application. The judge concluded that knowledge gleaned only from other members' written comments "must be deemed to be ignorance sufficient to preclude the exercise of any fair judgment upon the merits of the application." He then quashed the board's decision denying O'Brien's application and ordered the board to hold a new hearing with all voting members present.

The impact of these and related judgments on the way the parole board went about its business was profound. When the *Martineau* judgment imposed on the board the general "duty to act fairly" it's safe to say that many board members wrongly

assumed that they had always done so. Custom and conven-
ience and the arrogance that comes with power had made many
of our unfair attitudes and practices cozily acceptable. We were
ensconced more than we realized in an attitude of "us" versus
"them".

For instance, acting fairly required that a person know the
case against him, including all the information we had on file
relevant to the decision we would be taking. We were now
instructed by the board chairman to share all this file information with the inmate when the hearing began. This included
vital statistics; pattern of offences; any previous parole/
probation performance; the details of the present offence; criminal, family and social circumstances, education, and work
history; drug and alcohol use; institutional performance; and
release plans. We were then to end the information-sharing
session by stating the recommendations to grant or deny parole
that had been made by the prison staff member and the parole
officer.

Oh, how some of us groaned when we were told this!
"Impossible," we said, pointing to already overloaded schedules. "Our hearings will go on all night!" And, in fact, while
fairness was the intent the results were often demeaning. Having to raise often wretched family histories right at the beginning of the hearing, as well as other details of the inmates'
personal lives, which were usually riddled with failures at
school, jobs, and marriage, put the inmate in a vulnerable and
psychologically disadvantaged position. (This is not done
today; instead inmates are given this information in writing two
weeks before the hearing.)

After *Couperthwaite* our pre-hearing rap sessions were gone
forever. Furthermore, we were instructed not even to be seen
talking with prison staff members or parole officers without the
inmate being present, lest the appearance of fairness be jeopar-
dized. We were next told we had to notify the inmate if there
was confidential information in his file. For a few months we

got away with saying simply that, but then we were instructed that we were obligated under the Access to Information Act (1983) to share the "gist" of all confidential information with the inmate.

Of all the judgments handed down to the board this one seemed to us the most difficult to translate into practical terms. I recall one case, not untypical, in which an inmate's wife had informed us confidentially that her husband had threatened to have friends in the community "fix her" if she did not smuggle the drugs he wanted in to him. Sharing the "gist" of that type of information without endangering the informant required a lot of "talking slant". About a year later we were taken off the hook when another court ruled that, in cases where the lives or welfare of others could be endangered, it was sufficient for board members to inform the inmate that there was confidential information in his file.

The result of the *Dubeau* and *Morgan* cases, allowing for the provision of an "assistant" at all hearings, was received in our Ottawa office with a mix of grimness and hilarity. At that time Ottawa members were on the road two, three, and sometimes four weeks a month, flying from Dorchester, New Brunswick, to Kent, British Columbia, to the Saskatchewan Penitentiary in Prince Albert, and then down to Kingston. Often the cost precluded us from getting home for weekends, which were as often as not spent in some uninviting hotel or motel room. The idea of now having to cope with an inmate's weeping mother or belligerent wife or shattered father seemed like the last straw.

After the *Mason* and *O'Brien* rulings we could no longer do "paper" votes. In the case of lifers, this meant that seven rather than three members had to attend the hearing. Few prisons provide hearing-rooms big enough to accommodate seven board members. We spent several months at hearings virtually sitting on top of one another, along with the inmates and prison staff, until the regulations were changed to reduce the number of votes required to three. How the inmate felt when he entered the hearing-room and saw the grim line-up of seven board members huddled against the wall, all breathing in unison, can only be imagined.

Although I consider myself a fair person, I found myself very resistant initially to the notion that inmates were persons whose fundamental rights and freedoms were in no way threatened or diminished by the fact that they were in prison. However, as the various judgments were handed down and we put them into practice, my understanding and my thinking grew and changed, as, I am sure, did that of other board members. I came to fully appreciate the fact that the rule of law and the principle of fairness must operate inside the prison walls.

I believe that the key to maximizing the chances of an inmate being honest-to-God rehabilitated *starts* with giving him a sense of having basic rights and worth no matter what he has done. Without this feeling of worth, of still being a part of society even if he has offended against it, how can an inmate have the confidence, security, and motivation to co-operate and maximize his chances of rehabilitating himself? This assurance of fair treatment, backed by the highest courts in the land, is, I believe, at the core of any impetus to change.

The question of human rights is not an academic one as some tend to believe, but one that has value in human terms. In light of the current $1 billion spent annually on the federal system alone, this policy also offers tremendous economic value.

4   *The Sham of Rehabilitation*

Crime is not only expensive in terms of human victimization, suffering, and the general loss of quality of life; the dollar costs in managing its widespread results can bleed a society white. One would think that a comparatively humane and progressive penitentiary system such as we now have in Canada would be totally committed to sound rehabilitative programs that return the prisoner to society as a productive, law-abiding person.

This is not the case. Although enormous progress in humanitarian terms has been made since the brutalizing prison system of twenty years ago, there has never been a strong, clear, unflagging commitment to rehabilitation in Canadian prisons. There have been only half-hearted forays into the rehabilitative programs, incursions of sufficient duration and funding to enable old-timers in Correctional Service Canada to say: "We tried rehabilitation once and it didn't work."

Instead, there has been a commitment to building prisons, to creating "special handling units" for dangerous offenders, to making guards feel better about their wretched jobs by giving them tarted-up uniforms, to stepping up security — but never a comparable commitment to rehabilitation.

Rehabilitation programs do exist and some, like the adult basic education program in the Pacific region, are excellent. But many are mediocre. They depend on one overworked staff member whose training has been in other areas or on an outside volunteer, and as a result they frequently fold up. Too few programs address the greatest need of young inmates and some older inmates, which is training in trades.

Why this is so, I am not sure. It could be because a behemoth of a system like Correctional Service Canada can only move so far so fast. It could be because the bureaucrats in Ottawa are simply out of touch with the realities in the field. Or maybe it's just because rehabilitation requires an unshakeable belief that inmates *can* change, that there are ways of turning them around.

Even if you are committed to the possibility of change, even if your heart stays big enough to understand that despite their posturings most inmates don't like themselves the way they are, and that they can clearly see the mess they've made of their lives, working in or for a prison can wear out your optimism.

Prison inmates are, by and large, narcissists, adept at keeping others at a distance. To do this they employ an extensive reper- toire of psychological tricks. Cutting through these barricades to get to the core of their humanity takes an extraordinary amount of energy and time. First-class psychiatrists, psycholo- gists, and social workers are reluctant to work in prisons. And once they are hired it may be difficult to get them to stay. It's not only the inmates who grind the novices into the ground: it's equally the draining, bureaucratic demands made on these staff members by the Correctional Service.

The reason why penitentiary psychologists have little or no time left for inmates today is because, due to a policy change in July of 1986, inmates are now seen by the board at one-sixth, rather than one-third, of their sentence. The board requires a psychological assessment of the inmate for the review, leaving prison psychologists with little time for individual counselling; their main job has become one of writing assessments.

The value of such assessments in the case of prisoners doing short sentences of, say, two or three years is questionable, as such inmates are inside prison for less than four to six months when this assessment for parole is done. This barely allows enough time for the inmate to settle in, let alone provide sufficient time for the staff to know with whom they are dealing.

We also have to accept the uncomfortable fact that some inmates — in my opinion around 20 percent — don't *want* to change. They are either too old to bother or too young to understand that they're going down the fast lane on an unfinished bridge. Others cherish the image they have of themselves as thugs, *un homme de main*, while yet others simply don't see anything wrong with their behaviour. For these types even the best rehabilitation programs are money down the drain.

I agree with the experts who say that the brutal childhood experiences of many inmates have contributed to their anti-social attitudes. Influenced by poor living habits, skewed in their views of the world, profoundly wounded in their spirits, they have been "set up" by the accident of birth to become criminals. But I do not go as far as those who argue that all inmates' problems stem from their early years. I have too much respect for most inmates to believe that they don't have any free will, or that they are helpless, amoral zombies. Some psychologists, psychiatrists, sociologists, and criminologists have propounded this notion in the guise of an insightful, enlightened viewpoint when in fact it's just the opposite. It suggests that there is something terribly wrong with everyone who is in prison, that they are fundamentally different from the rest of us. This outlook is like saying that one race of people is less capable than another.

The majority of inmates who do want to change do not need more opportunities to bleed over their miserable childhoods. They need an understanding of who they are and where they are *now*, and a mastery of the techniques that will enable them to get on with the business of living. Once they've been given psychological help to deal with the past, access to a variety of solid rehabilitative programs, particularly trades training, is vital. This psychological help should be available very early in the sentence, when the full meaning of imprisonment first hits the strongest. As he becomes habituated to prison routine, his motivation to change fades.

When a judge hands out a prison sentence with the confident remark that once in prison the offender will receive the rehabilitative program that he obviously needs, the likelihood of the judge's prediction coming true is small. Because there are no system-wide goals and objectives regarding the rehabilitation of inmates, the types of programs available depend on the individual budget of each institution, on the availability of professional staff or outside personnel, and on the priority given to rehabilitation by each prison warden and staff. Existing programs are individually organized inside the Correctional Service's sixty-three institutions and many of these stop and start and change every few months, so it is not possible to give a cogent overview of what rehabilitative programs are available or their content. Asked at the time of this writing to provide such information, a senior official at Correctional Service Canada admitted that CSC itself did not have this information, but that the availability of rehabilitative programs was under study.

Over 80 percent of all crimes are drug- or alcohol-related, yet few competent addiction-control programs exist. One of them is at the Saskatchewan Penitentiary at Prince Albert, where the AA counsellor is skilled and highly experienced. Another is at Stony Mountain Penitentiary, outside Winnipeg. But in both cases individual therapy in the form of regular professional counselling is not widely available. At the Saskatchewan Penitentiary there are four hundred inmates, most of whom are violent offenders, and just two psychologists. At Stony Mountain there are three experienced psychologists, and an effective alcohol program that can only take forty inmates at a time. The prison has five hundred inmates, almost all of whom need this program.

At Drumheller there are four hundred inmates and one psychologist. Her time is totally consumed in doing assessments; individual counselling is out of the question. The badly needed life-skills program is run by a John Howard Society volunteer who comes in at night.

The accessibility to inmates of quality rehabilitative programs is a matter of chance. The alcohol- and drug-addiction program might be outstanding in one institution but the staff psychologist could be incompetent. In another institution there may be a good family-life improvement program that teaches better communication, budgeting, and parenting, but no trades training. Institutions that do offer trades training in areas like welding, carpentry, upholstery, auto mechanics, plumbing, and cooking never have enough places to satisfy the demand for them.

In most institutions, prison case-management staff, whose job it is to do case work and prepare viable release plans, have been turned reluctantly into therapists. They are ably running anger-management programs, alcohol programs, and drug-awareness programs, but this is not what they were employed to do.

The following composite cases summarize typical examples of how the shortage of rehabilitative programs is affecting inmates.

John Charles was a thirty-eight-year-old native in Stony Mountain Penitentiary. A ruddy-cheeked man, large and as strong as the proverbial ox, he had a record of violent assaults when under the influence of alcohol. This time he was serving six years for manslaughter. The victim was his wife, Josephine, thirty years old, mother of four of his six children. Josephine was badly beaten by her husband during a heavy drinking party one Christmas Eve. He tossed her out on the doorstep where she was found dead of exposure the next morning.

After serving a year at Stony Mountain, Charles was transferred to Bowden Institution in Alberta, to be near his relatives. Although both are medium-security institutions, Stony, a mouldy-looking fortress, is considered harder time.

In Bowden, Charles, who had been drinking since he was six and fighting for as long as he could remember, entered the drug-and-alcohol program and the anger-management program, which markedly improved his behaviour and attitude. Reports indicated that he enjoyed the anger-management program and was one of its most enthusiastic participants. Nevertheless, after a few months he got into a fight with another inmate and was transferred back to Stony Mountain, where he was put in the hole for three days.

The incident occurred ten months before Charles's application to the parole board for day parole. Charles had long since passed his full-parole eligibility date, but he had not applied for it, as he was a proud and intelligent man who was unwilling to risk rejection.

His day-parole application was based on a plan to enter the Phoenix program at the Alberta Hospital in Edmonton. This program dealt with anger and sexual aggression, which are often closely connected. The inmate was treated in the hospital and then escorted back into the community by a Phoenix program staffer. The next step was to allow him to return to the community unescorted, to practise what he had learned.

If the parole board voted to grant Charles his parole, they would be voting for a program that would eventually allow an inmate with a record of violence to return to the community on day parole totally unescorted. To the psychiatrists and therapists who ran the program, this solo step back into the community was an essential part of Charles's treatment. To the parole board, it was a question of balancing the risk to the community *now* against the risk to the community in a year's time if Charles went out untreated. Should anything go wrong — for instance, if Charles ran into an old buddy and started drinking — he was capable of extreme violence. If a "dangerous incident" occurred, the responsibility and the blame would be the parole board's, not the program organizers'. The "safe" action for the parole board would be to deny the day parole, and let Charles return to the community, untreated, on mandatory supervision.

On the other hand, all that Charles had done, except for the incident at Bowden, and all that he had said at the hearing, showed him to be an ideal candidate for the Phoenix program. Within the year he would reach his mandatory supervision date. This was his last chance to receive consistent — or for that matter any — rehabilitative treatment.

Had Charles been able to have regular sessions with any of the prison's three excellent psychologists since his return to Stony Mountain nearly a year earlier, the parole board would have had the information it needed to make a fully-informed decision. However, with three psychologists and five hundred inmates, Charles was still on the waiting-list. A psychologist had written the report required for Charles's hearing, but this assessment, based on a twenty-five-minute interview, could not provide the quality of information that would have come out of regular individual therapy.

The board members decided that, without an informed assessment based on observation over a long period, they could not justify the risk and so they denied Charles his day parole. He was released a year later, untreated, into the community.

Daniel Greysun, twenty-six, was another native in Stony Mountain. He came from a family that was highly respected by his band for sobriety and character. There were several band chiefs in his lineage, and all four of his siblings had had some form of post-secondary education. Two of them had received university degrees.

Greysun had an excellent reputation with the band. He normally did not touch alcohol and had no previous criminal record. But his only offence was serious. He had broken into a relative's house after drinking at a wedding celebration, abducted and raped his twelve-year-old female cousin. He had been sentenced to four years' imprisonment and had served nearly sixteen months of it.

Greysun was now eligible for full parole and wanted day parole to participate in the aggressive-behaviour-management clinic, organized by the Native Clan in Winnipeg. Like the Edmonton Phoenix program, the clinic was an excellent example of what can be done with community-based programs.

Although he had been more than a full year at Stony Mountain, Greysun had not yet been able to get into the alcohol program. He had seen a psychologist for twenty minutes on three separate occasions over the past four months. This psychologist did not perceive Greysun as a danger to society. He felt the "incident" was isolated, resulting directly from alcohol. Nonetheless, he assessed Greysun as having some psychosexual problems, and believed that he would benefit greatly from the aggressive-behaviour-management clinic.

The board voted for day parole to allow Greysun to participate. In so doing, the board knew that it was running counter to the opinion of some civil-libertarian lawyers who claim that, under the Charter of Rights and Freedoms, the board cannot grant day parole for treatment purposes only, because this is a form of coercion.

Aware that Greysun had received a total of sixty minutes of "rehabilitation" in the last year and a half, board members felt that the community's "rights" and Greysun's "rights" would both be better served by day parole "for treatment purposes only" — and let the chips fall where they may.

Lloyd Belonski, thirty-four, convicted three times for drug-trafficking, had served three years of a six-year sentence in Matsqui, B.C., and had applied for day parole to attend the Harbour Light (Salvation Army) twenty-eight-day residential substance-abuse program. He had twelve months to go before his mandatory release. He had finished his grade twelve during earlier sentences, had no stable employment record, and no specific trades training, even though he had spent eight of his adult years in prison. He had been a heroin user since the age of seventeen but claimed to have quit just before his last arrest.

The programs available to him were group transactional analysis, an assaultive-husbands program, life-skills, and the Matsqui alcohol program (MAP), which included any form of substance abuse. He had started MAP but had dropped out, claiming, "There was so much talk of the good times that we left there every time wanting to get stoned."

Board members greeted this claim with some scepticism. Statements like "I quit going to NA [Narcotics Anonymous] because half the guys there were stoned" are commonly made by inmates about various substance-abuse programs across the country, but it is virtually impossible for board members to get to the truth of the matter. After a time on the board, I decided that by and large inmates got out of these programs what they wanted to get out of them. MAP enjoyed a good reputation as a "starter" program, something that got a lot of inmates interested in pursuing more intensive treatment programs on the outside. (Even so, no statistics are available to indicate whether MAP really works or not.)

Board members noted that Belonski had twice been charged in prison with "being in a condition other than normal", he had been found guilty and lost several days of remission, a dubious start for someone wanting to be released from prison for treatment purposes. He admitted that he'd taken "a little Valium" but felt he deserved some credit as he had also been offered "something a lot stronger".

Alcohol and virtually all drugs are available in most Canadian prisons. More than four out of every five crimes today are drug- or alcohol-related, and demand for these substances by an addicted prison population is enormous. Alcohol, or "brew", is concocted from kitchen scraps and hidden in the most ingenious of places. Drugs of all sorts manage to find their way past the guards. There are some prison staff members who believe that the traffic could be stopped, but that it is tacitly allowed to keep the population "quiet".

Belonski was denied his day parole on the grounds that he had not changed his behaviour at all. Through his own unwillingness to make use of even the few programs offered, he had already been uselessly warehoused in Canadian prisons at taxpayers' expense for eight years.

Thomas Ryan, twenty, was seen at Mission prison in British Columbia's Fraser Valley. He was doing three years for break-and-enter on his first penitentiary term, and was seen at his full-parole eligibility date, after serving one year.

Ryan was a street kid, but an intelligent one with a grade twelve education. He'd left his foster home at sixteen and, although he wrote home from time to time, he had no close contact with his family. He had an earlier history of drug-taking, but said it was limited to marijuana, that it had never been "serious", and that he had quit using drugs even before coming to prison because he was "fed up with himself". He had started off as a cleaner in the institution, and now wanted to get into some sort of apprenticeship program outside the prison.

"More than anything I need a job," he said. "I don't want to be sloshing around with a mop four hours a day. I told my LUDO when I first came here that when I left I wanted to be qualified to get some sort of decent work. I've been scrounging around, mopping floors for a living all my life. Man, you can't live on money like that."

Asked how many B&Es he'd done, Ryan said six. A board member responded, "That's how many you've been charged with. How many have you actually *done*?" He replied, "Okay, I guess about forty, but I didn't like it. I was scared all the time I'd get caught."

Ryan explained that when he came into the prison he had asked for a course in auto mechanics, but two weeks later that course had been discontinued. He then asked to be allowed to take welding, and had waited three months to start the program when the instructor left. No replacement was found and that course also folded. He entered the furniture program and learned to upholster furniture. He didn't enjoy it but he had a job lead on the outside. What he really wanted to learn was still auto mechanics, perhaps at the British Columbia Institute of Technology (BCIT).

Ryan had no institutional charges against him and was regarded by prison staff as a likeable, straightforward young man. He was granted a six-month day parole to a halfway house that had already stated its willingness to accept him, on the condition that he continue to seek employment.

Ryan seemed to be thinking of his future, but it was unlikely that he would ever be able to go to BCIT. He had no money, no outside support. His one chance to make good had been in prison and the prison had failed to deliver.

Melvin Ratton, thirty-four, married with three children, was seen at Bowden Institution in Alberta. Fourteen years earlier, he had served eighteen months on a sexual assault charge. He was now doing five years for the rape of a sixteen-year-old hitch-hiker. He had served one year seven months and was approaching his full-parole eligibility date. His plan was to return home and resume his job as a truck driver. His wife was present as his assistant.

Ratton, like one-third of the Bowden population who were sex offenders, had never come forward to request treatment, partly because he did not want to risk being identified as a sex offender among the other inmates. He had done the family-life-improvement program and the drug-and-alcohol program, but he had done nothing that directly addressed his offence. His charge fourteen years ago indicated a long-standing psychosexual problem, and raised the question of what had been going on in the years between his first offence and his most recent one, which involved two young girls. (One of them had managed to jump out of his moving car, breaking her ankle.) I thought that even if Ratton had refused the program, in a segregated institution for sex offenders he would at least have had to cope with the fact that he was a sex offender. In Bowden, he could avoid this unpleasant reality. His attitude did little to reduce concern. He had told prison staff that the mere fact that the girls were out hitchhiking meant that they were "easy".

In the hearing, Ratton, now comfortably at his full-parole date and looking ahead to his mandatory release in less than two years, said he saw no need to participate in a sex-offender program. He had understood his "mistake" and had "made up his mind" that nothing like that would happen again. He said he had mistaken the girls' intentions.

Ratton was denied parole, and was strongly advised to reconsider his rejection of the specialized help he could receive from a six-month stay at the Regional Psychiatric Centre.

The above composite cases give a brief glimpse into some of the problems and complications associated with rehabilitation in the penitentiary system. I would summarize these as follows:

1. At least sixty more psychologists are needed to provide the individual therapeutic counselling that several thousand inmates need — and most want — as the first step to changing their lives.

2. Correctional Service Canada has failed to provide anything approaching adequate trades training, despite the fact that unemployability is one of the greatest problems faced by ex-inmates when they return to the street.

3. Substance-abuse programs in prison range from highly competent professional courses to amateur night in the confessional. Every prison should offer effective substance-abuse programs to all inmates.

4. The majority of sex offenders undergo no treatment whatsoever and are released back into the community untreated.

Only one hundred places in specialized treatment programs are available annually for over seven hundred of these offenders.

5. Society properly expects inmates to be more law-abiding when they leave prison than when they enter, but it does not understand the need to balance custody with programming. There are some cases in which society itself must choose between treatment with some risk while the offender is on partial release, and warehousing with no treatment and a greater risk on his final release.

6. Rehabilitative progress made in prison requires the development of, or contracting with, a variety of support systems in the community to ensure that progress is maintained and developed. Currently, insufficient efforts have been made towards creating community-based support programs.

There is no doubt in my mind that when someone is put into prison, particularly if that person is young, the penitentiary system has a superb opportunity to change his attitude towards himself and towards society. For at least two years, the system exercises control over that individual's every waking and sleeping hour. Millions of self-help books with hundreds of theories on how to make personal changes — many of them rubbish but some of them not — have been sold to the public in the last twenty-five years. Many people have made dramatic changes in their lives, their work, their ways of thinking, their diets, their goals and aspirations. Inmates are as capable of responding to different approaches to their problems, and of learning different techniques of living, as anyone else. But these types of programs seem to stop at the prison gate. All the rehabilitation programs put together would not cost as much as it now costs to build a few special handling units for violent offenders.

The long-term benefits of rehabilitation both to the offender and to the community are obvious. It is equally obvious that, without this commitment, the revolving door at each prison gate will continue to pump many of the same people in and out, generation after generation.

5   *The Assistant System*

In 1982 we were advised that all inmates would now be entitled to have an "assistant" at their hearings, a change that remains in effect today. This person could be anyone the inmate chose, former inmates excepted, as long as he or she passed the routine security checks.

Many inmates are edgy when they come up for a hearing. Some have spent the night before rehearsing in front of a mirror. Some play-act the hearing in their cells with a buddy. Occasionally a nervous inmate at a hearing either can't say a word or can't shut up. He leaves the hearing feeling that he did not have "a fair go". The presence of an assistant can boost his confidence and help avoid these situations.

An assistant can also provide another dimension to the hearing by revealing aspects of the inmate's character. A former boss, for instance, might have known the inmate as an excellent and reliable worker and be eager to get him back. A pastor might have known the inmate as a loving father and good provider for his family and be willing to arrange support for him on the outside.

The assistant is given a maximum of ten minutes at the end of the hearing to say whatever he or she wants to say. In 90 percent of cases board members have already made their decision on the inmate's application, and the assistant's statement is unlikely to influence them significantly. I've never seen the board release a gorilla because his mother thought he was an angel, but I do recall several cases where the decision was looking positive until the assistant unwittingly pulled the rug out from under the inmate. The case studies below illustrate the possible influence of an assistant.

David Edwards was forty when I met him in Dorchester Penitentiary, near Moncton. Edwards was a highly criminalized type. He was born in 1944, the oldest of three boys in a policeman's family in the Alymer region of Quebec. His record started in 1961 with four charges of B&E and theft, and two counts of damage. He was sentenced to an indefinite period in reform school in Ontario. Released a year later, he was arrested shortly after for housebreaking with intent, resulting in a six-month sentence in the provincial institution at Guelph. By 1965 Edwards was in Kingston Penitentiary serving a two-year sentence for robbery. Following a disturbance there, he was transferred to the British Columbia Penitentiary in New Westminster, which is now closed.

In 1968 Edwards, who had started to use heroin, pulled his first armed robbery. By the time he was picked up he had committed five such robberies. The total charges — five counts of armed robbery, six charges of conspiracy, one charge of assault with intent, two charges of possession of a weapon, and one charge of wearing a mask — earned him a total of eleven years in prison. After serving six years Edwards, now thirty, was released on a gradual parole program.

In prison, Edwards had taken a bricklaying course. On the outside, he found a demand for his services and, as he was to say later, "the pleasant realization that I could have a normal life". Sometime during this period he formed a friendship with Murielle Moen, who worked for the same Montreal bricklaying company as bookkeeper.

After two years with the company, he and some other employees were laid off in a mini-recession. For a time Edwards looked for work locally while he lived off his savings; eventually he continued his job search while moving around the country.

His job, his skills, the routine of working, getting a pay envelope: for a time these things seemed to build a wall between Edwards and crime. They created the image of a changed man, but Edwards's fundamental attitudes hadn't changed. Once he lost his job his immaturity and irresponsibility resurfaced, and in early 1977 Edwards did a swan dive back into crime.

By late 1977 he was serving eight years on one count of armed robbery and one count of possession of a sawed-off rifle, plus the unexpired portion of his sentence of 1968, about three years and ten months.

In late 1984 Edwards applied for day parole. He had long passed his full-parole eligibility date but had waived a hearing, well aware that his horrendous record would preclude any serious possibility of early release.

Edwards was a man of striking good looks, brown-haired, even-featured, tanned, with even white teeth and blue eyes. He moved like an athlete across the room and introduced his assistant, Murielle Moen, with the smiling confidence of a successful businessman, graciously gesturing to her to sit down.

Murielle Moen appeared to be about forty, intelligent and fit, although no beauty. A mass of carroty hair was piled on her head, she wore thick glasses, small pearl earrings, and no makeup other than lipstick. She was dressed in a prim grey suit with a high-collared white blouse. A fourth-timer, Edwards was extremely con-wise, able to present himself in the most favourable light possible. I wondered if Ms. Moen were part of the scenario he'd dreamed up to impress the board.

Edwards's release plan was to go to Sherbrooke Community Correctional Centre, a halfway house in downtown Montreal, where the director was prepared to accept him. The Montreal police had been contacted by the parole service — normal procedure with serious offenders — and had no objection to his release. Edwards planned to go back to bricklaying but as yet he had no job.

CSC reports told us a lot that we already knew from older files. "Subject comes across as a highly intelligent individual. He rationalizes extremely well. Has not been outside for over seven years but has managed to maintain a positive attitude. He has had no institutional offences since 1982, has had no escorted absences and has received few visits. He maintains a number of contacts by letter, including his former parole officer."

A brief psychological assessment by the prison psychologist stated, "There has been a marked evolution in his ability to control his impulses. There is no evidence of any aggressive tendencies. Subject was open and frank in discussion. There was no indication of thought or perceptual disorder. Has average or normal conscience function."

I made a note to myself that all these points had also been made prior to Edwards's 1974 release.

My colleague, whom I'll call Tom, was leading the case and he started off by pointing out to Edwards that there was little in the present reports that had not been in the earlier reports.

"You present yourself well, you have a good release plan, you express good intentions — and when things go wrong you go right back to it." Tom paused for a moment. "I notice in the police report that the rifle was loaded. Is that correct?"

"Yes," said Edwards. He did not add that he had no intention of using it, which some inmates are fool enough not only to say but also to believe.

"In our view, Mr. Edwards, that makes you a dangerous person and a potential risk. Your record goes back twenty-three years."

"Yes," said Edwards again. Ms. Moen sat as still as a piece of porcelain on a mantel.

"So what is there to stop the same thing happening this time when things go wrong, as they do to everyone on occasion?"

"That won't happen," said Edwards. He spoke quietly but intensely. "I'd like to tell you what really happened last time."

Tom nodded. "Go ahead, it's your hearing."

Edwards edged his chair closer. "I was in prison last time from age twenty-four to thirty. Before that I was in provincial jails. From the time I was seventeen I was locked up. I should have been. My dad told me I was a no-good bum when I was fourteen and he was right! My life so far proves it. Being in jail so much though . . . well, I identified with it. Even the last time I was in, I felt part of the place, sort of at home, not so much as the earlier sentence but, still, when I got my parole last time I felt I was leaving something I knew for something I didn't know. I knew how to survive in prison but I really didn't know how to survive outside.

"But then things worked out. It was great. I liked getting a paycheque. I never thought I'd like going to work every morning, but I got used to it. My boss liked the work I did. I didn't think there was much to bricklaying but some guys are sloppy and slow. And then I met Murielle."

He hesitated. "One of the things that happens when you're locked up so long is, well, you don't know what's happened to you as a man. You don't know whether you'd ever be normal enough to be able to love someone or for someone to love you. You don't know about sex — I mean, what you'd be like, whether you'd be any good or not. So much goes on inside prison. . . . Since I was a kid in the juvenile homes I've seen things that would shock people on the outside, but here you get used to it. It's normal."

Again he paused. "Then, as I said, I met Murielle. I was made a supervisor after a year and I had to go into the office quite a bit, and we got to know one another, and started going together. I didn't know I could ever feel that way, I mean so like other people, ordinary people. I'd been in and out of prison for about fifteen years and it was a sort of home to me. That's where all my friends were. I never thought I could just have a normal life, like being happy, having a job, not have anyone giving you orders all the time, and I never thought I'd feel good about myself, or have someone like Murielle."

He looked at her as he said this, then stopped talking for a moment, his mouth a tight line, as he fought for self-control.

"Then," he said, "I got fired, laid off, whatever you call it. It wasn't only me, lots of the guys did. It was a seniority thing. Last hired, first fired. It hurt a lot but my boss gave me good references. I thought I'd get another job right off but the construction industry had gone belly-up. Murielle and I . . . things started to come apart. She kept her job and I got tossed out. I couldn't stand it not to pay my own way, so I cleared out and looked for work in other parts of Quebec, then Ontario, and finally ended up in New Brunswick.

"One day I passed a bank. And that afternoon I came back and just did it. It was the most goddamned stupid thing I've ever done in my life."

In the pause that followed I said, "The way you've put it sounds as if there was no planning at all. But you came back with a rifle, a loaded sawed-off rifle. Where did you get it?"

"Contacts," he said.

"I want to clear up a point while we're here," I said to Tom, then turned back to Edwards. "I presume these contacts were fellows you'd known on the inside? Okay. You knew you were taking a risk getting back with the same crowd into that same old scene again."

"I didn't have any other friends. When you're in most of your life the only people you know are ex-cons. I knew it was risky. I thought as soon as I got a job I'd get out of it and get my life together again. But" — he waved his hand — "the cops picked me up an hour later. And I've been here since.

"Two years ago, after I'd done five years, I decided I'd try and contact Murielle. I figured she'd probably be married or something by then, but I wanted her to know why I walked out the way I did, and what happened to me after. We'd gotten right out of touch. I'd made up my mind I wouldn't write a line to her until I'd found a job. But I never did.

"Well, Murielle wrote back, and we've been writing ever since. We want to get married. I've done seven years straight: I haven't asked for any passes, nothing. I'm burned out. I'm forty years old, my hair's beginning to go grey, I'm not a kid anymore. I'm fed up with prison, fed up with all this crap, fed up with all the bullshit in places like this. I want out, I want a chance."

We were silent for a moment, absorbing his words and all the emotion that had come with them. They seemed to be straight from his heart, but who could tell? Perhaps he had said something similar ten years ago. The notion of "burning out" was convincing. It happened to many inmates when they saw their first grey hairs and looked at their lives and their bank accounts and saw how little a life of crime had given them.

I had another question: "In the police report of the offence there's no mention of you wearing a mask or covering your head."

"That's right, I didn't."

"That seems strange, an odd risk for a pro like you to have taken."

He responded quickly that he'd thought a lot about that in the last few years. "This'll sound crazy, but I think I wanted to get caught. I've tried to remember what my feelings were, I don't really remember, but I think I felt like I should get caught. Like prison's a home for me. I belonged here."

Tom said, "The same feeling might drive you back here again."

Edwards shook his head slowly, emphatically. "It's finished. I've got nothing. I don't have any money, I don't have a wife, I don't have kids, a house, a car, a job, nothing."

"I hear what you're saying. I've no doubt you could go straight and make it if you wanted to. The question is: do you want to?" At that Tom turned to Murielle Moen. "If you have anything you'd like to say, Ms. Moen, you have ten minutes in which to do so."

Moen, who'd been sitting up straight and prim as the old hard-backed chair she sat in, went into action. From a brief-sized shoulder-strap purse she pulled out a series of documents and placed them on the table. "These are financial statements and personal references for your perusal, if you wish," she said in a clear, brisk voice. "Now, as to David. You're probably wondering if I'm a naive woman, closing my eyes to the facts for the sake of marriage, wondering, in fact, if I know what I'm getting into."

She paused while her words sunk in. The board members were all sitting up by this time as primly as the lady herself, struck silent by her unexpected, and accurate, analysis.

"I assure you I know perfectly well what I am doing. You have read David's records. I know all about them myself. But I know David. When he says he is burned out it's because he *is* burned out. I have sounded him out very thoroughly as to his future plans and I am of the strong opinion he should be given this opportunity.

"I have worked with the same company for twenty years. I have had only myself to look after and have done very well financially. In fact, I am now half-owner of the sub-contracting company for which David worked. In five years' time, my partner will be retiring and I intend to take over the whole company — if things go as I plan and I see no reason why they won't."

Holy crowley! I thought. This is one tough lady.

She continued: "I want David to help me run the business. I could do it alone, but I'd prefer to share it. There is nothing wrong with David's intelligence, misused it though he has."

At this point Edwards turned to her and smiled the idiotic smile of a man in love. The board members were staring at the two players as if they were at Wimbledon waiting for the next volley.

"He's also an excellent and reliable worker. He knows all there is to know about bricklaying, supplies, ordering, and his standards are high. I want him, and I want him now, as it will take a couple of years for him to get back completely into the swing of things." Leaning forward, she pushed the papers on the desk across to us. "This gives you my total worth. My stockbroker's number and the bank manager's number are there should you wish to refer to them."

Tom jumped in: "Ms. Moen, we appreciate the information you've provided but we are more concerned with the stability and quality of the relationship than your finances. What would you do, for instance, if you thought David was returning to crime?"

"If you don't mind, I'll address that question later. Now, as to David, I plan to marry him. I am thirty-nine years old. I have never married. I want to have a child. David wants to marry and he also wants a child. If I am to have a child it must be soon; my time is running out. The whole arrangement suits David and me. I know all there is to know about him and his past. We are not teenagers. This arrangement might not be conventional but it suits us. In preparation, David and I have had a marriage contract drawn up."

With this she held out a document and Tom, absolutely astonished, accepted it wordlessly. "Now, as to what I would do if I thought David was slipping, I would contact his parole officer immediately. You see," she concluded, looking at all of us full-faced, "it means much more to me than it could possibly mean to you for David to make it."

She gave a smile that lit up her face. "That is all I wish to say."

We gave Edwards a full parole. We did not believe that he had changed completely, or that the criminal impulses that had ruined his life had totally disappeared. But it wasn't necessary that they had. His ability and determination to live within the law, even if he still had some innate crooked impulses, was the bottom line. We accepted his word that he was burned out, that prison was no longer home to him, and that for some time he had tasted the bitterness of having nothing as a direct result of crime. We felt that if anyone could keep him straight, Murielle Moen was that person. Marriage to her was going to be like a life on mandatory supervision.

Ray Melling, thirty-six, was serving three years for incest. The victim was his twelve-year-old stepdaughter, Becky. Melling was the oldest of six children. He described his home life as average, although other reports stated that he was often severely beaten by his father, a strict disciplinarian who believed the eldest son should be beaten into conforming shape as an example for the younger children to follow. He maintained contact with his parents and with his two brothers and three sisters.

Melling had gone to public school in Winnipeg, and partially completed grade nine. He had had no significant school problems. He left home at fifteen and worked as a general labourer in construction. Over the years he had gained skills as a backhoe-operator, driller, and blaster.

At twenty-two he married Gloria Allen, who bore him two sons. They were later divorced. When questioned by the PO in preparing his parole recommendation, Melling was vague as to the reasons. He admitted his drinking was a contributing factor. He did not support the children and did not know his ex-family's whereabouts, although he had heard they were living in Sudbury, Ontario. At twenty-seven Melling married his current wife, Thelma. Thelma was then the single mother of a three-year-old girl. At the time Melling was employed as a backhoe-operator for a construction company in Winnipeg.

At 95, Melling's IQ was in the dull normal range. Although he had expressed willingness to get involved in a therapeutic program at the beginning of his sentence, he had to wait some months for an appointment and by then was no longer willing, stating that the shame he had experienced was more than sufficient to control his behaviour in the future.

The police report on file stated that between June 1979 and April 1982 Melling had had sexual intercourse with his step-daughter approximately twenty times against her will. The first offence occurred when the child was nine. At the age of twelve she confided in a school friend, who told her own mother. The mother in turn informed the police. Evidence came out during the trial that the victim had been subject to various forms of sexual assault, such as fondling and touching, by her stepfather since the age of five.

The inmate's version of the offence was different in part from the police report. Melling did not deny the offence, but he stated that it had occurred only four or five times. He denied the allegations of earlier sexual assaults, saying that it was his habit to bathe and dry Becky and that she had exaggerated and dis-torted matters. He said he had ceased bathing her at age nine. Furthermore, he said that he had never forced Becky to engage in intercourse, nor had he ever threatened her.

Various reports on Melling's attitude towards the offence were confusing. When questioned by his PO he wept copiously and admitted his aberrant sexual behaviour. He expressed great shame and confusion, and blamed his excessive drinking, his wife's "frigidity" and her failure to meet his sexual needs. He added that Becky had not seemed upset, nor had she ever complained to anyone about their relationship. Although he felt great shame when the matter became public, he did not feel that he had in any way harmed his stepdaughter.

Melling was applying to enter a temporary-absence program that would allow him to go home for thirty-six hours every second weekend. He and his wife owned a neat bungalow in one of the north-western suburbs of Winnipeg. Since his imprisonment Thelma had obtained a job in a dry-cleaning establishment in a shopping-centre close to their home. As the family had no debts, a low mortgage rate and no transportation costs, Mrs. Melling had managed to survive without applying for public assistance.

Melling had been assessed by a psychiatrist before the hearing. The gist of this lengthy but not particularly enlightening report was that Melling was pleasant and co-operative during the interview and did not deny the offences. There was no evidence of any mental illness or mental deficiency. He was not a man for discussions of an analytical nature, although he could have benefited from intensive one-to-one counselling. He came across as someone with a lifelong poor self-image and low self-esteem. Asked about alcohol use, he admitted that he resorted to alcohol when he was feeling "down". Melling was probably far more dependent on alcohol than he realized. He admitted that he had committed most of the offences when he was drinking.

The report concluded:

> Mr. Melling's use of alcohol is probably extensive. His experience of rejection by his wife, and his frustrated sexual needs, resulted in heavy, although perhaps secret, drinking within the home. The combination of the disinhibiting effects of alcohol on sexual impulses, plus the proximity of his stepdaughter, resulted in the offences.
>
> I cannot predict the specifics of his future behaviour but, if he agrees to continued involvement with AA and outside family counselling, see no reason why he could not be granted a parole.

We also had in our files the remarks of the sentencing judge. It is common practice for the regional offices of the board to obtain the judge's sentencing remarks for inclusion in the file before an inmate's hearing. This is not done in routine cases such as break-and-enter, but is usually done in cases of violence and of sexual assault, and where longer sentences are handed out. Sometimes the court sets out its intent in sentencing very clearly, which is a great help to the board members in difficult cases, and sometimes the court does not. When the sentencing remarks of a judge are requested, the judge will often write an accompanying letter to the board. Even if the case had been heard many years earlier, it was surprising to me how clearly many judges recalled the details, the issues, the particular "ambience" that made this case different from the hundreds of cases he or she had sat on since.

In Melling's file the judge's sentencing remarks were brief:

> I have read the psychiatric reports and the other exhibits that were presented on the accused's behalf. This is an offence which carries with it a maximum penalty of fourteen years' imprisonment. Various courts of appeal decisions seem to say that the penalty should run between two and seven years. The offences we are looking at today are neither the least nor the worst. The sentence must reflect the community's response, and in this instance we notice a fair amount of community support for the defendant. Several neighbours of good character have testified to his stability and willingness to be a responsible, co-operative neighbour; his employer is anxious to have him back; and the church to which he belongs testified to his established role as a faithful attendant.
>
> The sentence must also reflect the protection of others, and in this respect we note it is not a matter of community concern but one of a particular family. Mr. Melling cannot be considered a danger to society in the normal sense. We must also reflect in our sentence rehabilitation and deterrence, specific and general deterrence. I am therefore sentencing you to three years.

The remarks gave no clear or specific intent as to the future handling of the case. Even the remark on rehabilitation was a general consideration. In addition, we had a pile of letters from members of the community. I never ceased being surprised at how some communities rallied around men convicted of incest. There was a recent letter from Melling's former boss, another from a co-worker, one from the pastor of his church, and three from male fellow members and their wives. All the letters were the same in that they did not mention the twelve-year-old victim; it was as if she did not exist.

However, we also had a letter from the victim herself. In large, round lettering it read: "My Dad will soon be having a hearing to see if he can come home to us or not. I want him to come home. Dad and I have spoken about what happened and it is all in the past. I visit Daddy every Sunday. We are all lonely and miss him. He is a good father and I want him home. Yours truly, Becky."

I read the letter through once, twice, trying to get a "feel" from it. Had it been her idea to write it or had it been dictated?

Melling had passed his full parole date six months earlier. Because of the comparative brevity of his sentence, he would be released on MS in another six months. A request for an unescorted temporary-absence program to spend every second weekend at home was a modest one at this stage of sentence. He had applied six months earlier but the board had refused, saying that he had undergone no therapy, had no insight into his offence, and should join AA to gain control of his drinking problem. Up-to-date reports indicated he had taken the board at its word and had faithfully attended AA meetings. He had seen the prison psychologist on one occasion, and was now claiming he had an understanding of why he committed his offences.

Melling and his wife entered the hearing-room and, after preliminary introductions, sat down. He was a surprisingly large man, dark-haired and brown-eyed: all the talk of low self-image, low self-esteem had led me to expect a weedy little guy. Mrs. Melling looked older than her husband. Her skin was pale, her grey hair streaked blonde, her mouth a thin sunken line over a small rounded chin. Silently, she eyed the board with barely concealed resentment.

We were dealing with a very disagreeable offence, for which the sentence was three years, meaning a two-year maximum and one year on mandatory supervision. Eighteen months of that two years had passed and in six months Melling would be released anyway. Meanwhile he had refused to be involved in any systematic therapy for sex offenders, claiming that shame, attendance at AA, and a new understanding of his offence would preclude any recurrence.

"What is this new understanding you have, Mr. Melling?" I asked.

"Well, it's like this," he said, while his wife glared around the room, "I only got involved in that business when I'd been drinking. So if I quit drinking, it won't happen."

"Why were you drinking so much, Mr. Melling?" I asked.

He looked acutely uncomfortable. "I really don't want to talk about it. That's between my wife and myself."

"You might not want to talk about it," I said, "but as it was one of the factors involved in your committing the offences, we want to hear about it."

He sat looking at his hands, while his wife stared at him. Finally, he glanced at her and said in a rush, "There wasn't any sex between us. I wanted it, but she wouldn't. So I started drinking because I felt all tensed up. And then, a few times Becky was home . . . and it happened."

"Did you drink and then think about Becky, or did you think about Becky and then get drunk?" I asked. No answer. "Where was your wife when this was going on?"

"Out shopping, or at church meetings."

"What have you learned from this experience, Mr. Melling? What can you say that might convince us that Becky will not be assaulted by you again, and that you're not going to be a risk to anybody else?"

I didn't expect illuminating self-analysis. I was looking for something that would indicate he feared coming back to jail, or feared losing his family, or felt so remorseful that he would seek outside help to keep the family together — or that he at least accepted responsibility for his own acts.

Instead he gave a nervous laugh: "Well, for one thing I can't stand this place." He stared off into the distance: "And I wish none of this mess had ever happened."

I turned to my colleagues. "Do you have any questions?" They shook their heads. It seemed a straightforward decision. His wife wanted him home, the prison records showed Becky visited regularly just as her letter claimed, the church community wanted him back, and so did his boss. He had served most of his sentence and would not benefit from further incarceration. He had as much insight into his problems as he was likely ever to get. Becky was now over fourteen years of age and knew that the law was on her side, and her mother, now alert to the situation, would obviously protect her. Melling had his UTA program in the bag.

Then I turned to Mrs. Melling. "Would you like to add anything, Mrs. Melling?"

"Yes, I would," she said. "I've been married to Ray for eleven years. He's a good worker, a good man. He goes to church, just ask anyone there. They'll tell you that Ray Melling is all right. We've got a nice house, there's no reason why he should stay here."

Her voice started to tremble and the thin line of her mouth to wobble. I waited for tears but none came. I realized she was quivering with rage, not sorrow.

"No reason at all he should be here. It's not him, you know, what should be here. It's that little bitch. She's the one the police should have picked up and put in jail. She's the one that should have been crying and shamed for eighteen months, not my Ray. She led him into it. She was always that way, wasn't she, Ray?" — she tossed a glance at her husband who nodded in vigorous agreement — "dancing around in her little panties when she was three and four, flirting and acting that way even then, the little bitch!"

"Did you make her write that letter, Mrs. Melling?" I asked.

"No, I didn't," she said. "And I didn't make her come here to see him either."

"Was there any discussion between the two of you about coming here, or writing?"

"I don't know what you mean 'discussion'. I didn't make her come here, if that's what you mean. Although after all the trouble and misery she's caused it's the least she could do, the little tramp."

Carried away by spite and rage, and probably some deeply felt grief, Thelma Melling revealed the extent of the pathology in that family. Ray Melling's nodded agreement to Thelma's charge that Becky had acted provocatively as a toddler — shifting blame to the child for the rape that followed a few years later — showed his perception of himself as the victim in the whole affair.

We realized that if we refused to grant a release to Melling, the relationship between his wife and daughter would probably further deteriorate, but both the board and Melling's PO and LUDO felt that Melling still represented some degree of risk to his stepdaughter. Before he was released family-therapy resources in the community should be contacted with the hope that Mrs. Melling whose alleged "frigidity" had supposedly contributed to the situation in the first place, could receive some marital counselling (perhaps with her husband) and that Becky would have the professional supports she needed before and after her stepfather came home. If the Mellings refused to become involved in therapy, there was nothing the board, or any other agency, could do.

Melling was denied his request for an unescorted temporary absence.

Although there had been some initial resistance by board members, the presence of an assistant soon became a routine part of the hearing process. Although the two examples above illustrate the type of contribution an assistant can make, the normal contribution, if any, is minimal.

There is one potential inequality in the system. As stated

earlier, lawyers can also act as assistants. Inmates with money, such as members of organized crime, can afford the best. Arguments for their release are more cogently presented than those by other inmates' family members or friends. This inequality is an inescapable part of the court system, but I always thought it a shame to extend it into the parole system.

6   *The Women Who Wait*

When a man is sentenced to prison there is often a woman in the background who is sentenced along with him — not to prison but to something akin to a prisoner's life. From the moment the judge pronounces sentence, her life, too, is under the control of the criminal justice system.

The type of prison her mate or relative is in, the number of visits he is allowed, the times of visiting, the accessibility of transportation to the prison, whether it's close to a major city or in the wilds: she has no control over these factors, yet they will dominate her life. When he is transferred to another prison in another province, she will probably move to be near him. When he is transferred back, she may again relocate. When he is granted a pass or parole, she will provide the apartment or home for him to come to. Until he can support himself, she will provide the meals he eats, the clothing he wears, the entertainment he enjoys, and the transportation he needs.

Who are these women? There are over twelve thousand male inmates in Canada's penitentiaries and most of them have a woman who is waiting — a wife, mother, girlfriend, sister, daughter, or sometimes a grandmother or aunt. If she is close to the inmate and has no police record, Correctional Service Canada and the National Parole Board will likely regard her as the inmate's single most valuable community resource.

Many of these women have little money, and providing for the inmate's needs often strains a budget already stretched to the breaking point. They find it even more difficult to cope with the lack of rehabilitation programs inside the prison and the expectation, often tacitly expressed at hearings by staff and board members, that once the inmate is outside *they* can make up for the failures of the criminal justice system, by providing consistent patience, understanding, and support.

Society seems to rely on the adage that "the love of a good woman is the making of a man", placing part of the responsibility for an ex-inmate's success or failure onto the woman's shoulders, while diminishing the accountability of the criminal justice system for its failure to rehabilitate or deter. If this is so, then we credit the woman with powers and capacities that the entire billion-dollar prison system lacks. Yet, even while a woman's ability to rehabilitate a man is upheld, the mere fact that she is involved with an inmate demeans her in the eyes of many, who ask, "What sort of woman has anything to do with an inmate?"

The answer, to a large extent, is ordinary women with middle-class values, rather than "street" values. Women with "street" values usually don't have much staying power: they find it particularly hard to do their husband's or boyfriend's time. They miss the good times they had before, they dislike the discipline imposed by prison visiting and the proximity of prison authorities, and they resent the demands made on them by their incarcerated husbands or boyfriends. They often use drugs, previously supplied by their husbands or boyfriends, and move on to new suppliers. Furthermore, if they themselves have a record, or are known to do drugs, permission to visit will likely be denied. If it is granted, these women will be subject at random to body searches, a degrading process for anyone.

The women who are still hanging in when parole time comes around are often those who believe in the value of a home, of working hard, raising children, and being generally responsible in their neighbourhoods and communities. They are not opposed to authority and usually they feel their men deserved a prison sentence, although they often don't agree with its duration. (It is doubtful that any intelligent person, once they know prisons as well as these women do, would agree with lengthy sentencing.)

They have been helped to endure the term by the introduction of private family visits (PFVs), or "conjugal visits", as they were called when they were first introduced in the early 1980s. These PFVs take place in a large mobile home, with a backyard and surrounded by a high fence, which is within the prison walls but set apart from the regular prison. Families, or couples who qualify, are entitled to seventy-two hours together every two months, or forty-eight hours one month and twenty-four the next. In my opinion, this program has been the single most successful initiative introduced into the prison system in the last two decades.

Sharon Dimatina was working as a volunteer at a shelter for battered women in the Toronto area when I met her. She was a well-groomed twenty-four-year-old, athletic and trim in a sweatsuit, wearing pink-tinted glasses and soft, muted makeup. She told me she was the wife of an inmate at Warkworth Institution, near Trenton, Ontario, and that she worked at the shelter one day a week. She said that she was on welfare, and shared an apartment with another inmate's wife. Each had one child, both aged two. The two women babysat for each other, juggling schedules while they attended Ryerson Polytechnical Institute, Dimatina taking a legal secretarial course and her friend a medical secretarial course.

Sharon told me she was twenty when she married Joe Dimatina against her parents' wishes. Her family lived in Brampton, Ontario, west of Toronto, and had traditional values. Her father was an accountant and her mother had trained as a nurse before her marriage. Sharon was the younger of two daughters. The older girl, Diane, had become a registered nurse.

Sharon met Joe when she was eighteen and planning to return to school to become a dental hygienist.

Joe was ten years older than Sharon and they met jogging in the local park. Although she was not all that keen at first, Sharon was flattered that a handsome "older" man, more experienced and sophisticated, was taking such an interest in her. Joe was both persistent and persuasive, and before long the two were meeting regularly.

Sharon hesitated to take Joe home to meet her parents: she intuitively knew that they would not approve of him. This made her angry, an anger that she tried to suppress but which burst through in a series of small spats with her parents about unrelated matters. When her parents finally guessed that she had been going with someone, they correctly concluded that she was reluctant to bring him home because she knew they would disapprove of the relationship. By the time Sharon brought Joe home they disliked him thoroughly. His added ten years, and the fact that he had been previously married and divorced, did nothing to improve their attitude.

"My dad started saying things like 'As long as you're under this roof and I pay all the bills you'll do as you're told,'" recalled Sharon. "As if I was fifteen! And then mum would start in: 'I don't know what you see in him, with all the other nice young men around.' I don't know what happened, because until then my parents and I had been really close. It was as though all that closeness had been false, it all just disappeared. Poof, it was gone.

"Actually, I had my own doubts about Joe. He could get really loud and I always felt, like, nervous, or a bit scared when he'd been drinking. And he was very jealous. Once he saw me downtown with Diane's husband, Steve, my brother-in-law, but he didn't know who it was, and when we met later he was really strange. What I didn't like about it was that he didn't say anything about seeing me downtown. He just kept asking me what I'd being doing that day, and who I'd seen. I felt that was kind of sly. I'd forgotten I'd run into Steve so I didn't mention it. Finally, I found out what he was going on about, and he made me get Steve on the phone so that he could talk to him. Diane didn't like it one bit: she said Joe was too jealous, but I believed him when he later said that it just meant he loved me a lot.

"Just about the time I was having second thoughts my parents gave up, and said they didn't like it, but they wouldn't stand in my way if I insisted on marrying him. So I got all caught up in that, and had a big church wedding. And then a month after we were married, Joe beat me up."

Sharon jerked her head up, keeping in check the few tears that had sprung spontaneously into her eyes. Even though the assault had happened three years earlier, the memory still unloosed a lot of pain. Brushing her fingertips across her eyes, she continued.

"He'd been back at work only two days — he was a computer programmer — and I was sitting on the floor unpacking some of our wedding gifts. I didn't hear him until he'd turned the key in the lock and stepped inside. I looked up and beamed as he strode over to me." Sharon paused again to gain control.

"And then he just struck me, hauled back and struck me. I don't mean, like, he slapped me, I mean he felled me." She stopped and waved her hand in front of her body, as if trying to keep at bay memories too painful to contemplate. After a moment she said, "I don't remember anymore. When I woke up I was on the bed and he was kneeling beside it crying and asking me to forgive him. I couldn't understand what had happened. I didn't know anything about battered wives. I don't think my dad ever hit my mum once during their whole marriage, and I can't imagine Steve hitting Diane.

"Anyway, I cried all night, and he kept saying he was sorry, and he didn't know why it had happened, but it would never happen again. I stayed in bed in the morning and pretended I was asleep and Joe went off to work without waking me. When

I saw my face in the mirror. . . . Well, they say things don't actually break your heart, but the day before I'd gotten our wedding pictures back and the difference" — Sharon's voice quavered — "well, I really did feel my heart was broken. I just couldn't understand why he'd done it. I didn't know that he believed this was the way wives were supposed to be treated.

"Mum and dad were supposed to be coming over for dinner that night, but I called and said I had the flu, and would they mind coming a few days later. Mum said she would pop by and help me — I could tell she was really looking forward to coming — and I just felt awful but I had to insist she didn't come. I got really sharp with her and could tell it hurt her a lot, but it was because they'd never liked Joe, and there was no way I could let her see me like that. My whole face was bruised. I wanted desperately to tell someone about it, but on the other hand I couldn't bear to. I felt so ashamed.

"A couple of months later I happened to read an article on battered wives in *Chatelaine*. I didn't think I came into that category at all — I thought maybe I'd done something to trigger it — but I still wanted to talk to someone about it. Without telling Joe I phoned the local hospital and the local mental-health services to see if there was some sort of program we could go to together, because for a while after it happened I felt like I was in a bad dream. But there wasn't anything, and as time went by and things were okay I figured I'd exaggerated it all and it had been a really freaky sort of single incident and it would never happen again.

"About nine months went by, and I was about four months' pregnant. I'd been at mum's this day and Joe dropped by to pick me up. I was in a maternity outfit for the first time. It was cute and mum said I was just glowing. I was hoping he'd say something nice about it, but he just strode in, glanced at it, and told me to get my coat. He was really tense, different from himself, and I just wished he hadn't been like that in front of mum.

"When we got out to the car I said, 'What's the matter,

darling?' He clutched the wheel and told me to shut up. I didn't say anything until we were back home again. I asked him again what was the matter. I really wanted him to be able to confide in me. But what he did was take me by the shoulders and shake me like crazy and scream at me to shut up! I screamed back and he slapped me full across the face. Hard. I ran into the bedroom and locked the door.

"After a while he asked me to let him in. I wouldn't at first but he kept begging and saying he was sorry, so after a couple of hours I let him in, and he apologized and swore it would never happen again. I told him straight that if it ever did, I'd leave him for sure. He knew that my parents had never liked him, and that I'd sort of defied them by marrying him, and maybe he was counting on me not leaving him because of that, because of my pride, or maybe he really honestly believed it would never happen again.

"The thing that's so hard to explain is that Joe is really a good man. Maybe the marriage wasn't ideal, but we had grown closer. It was actually working. I'm a domestic kind, quite happy at home, and he's enough of a male chauvinist to like having me at home. He seemed proud of me and loved to take me out, and we'd made some friends in common, and I think you could say both of us in our own way were working at it. But I'd made up my mind to leave him if he ever knocked me about again, because soon I was going to have a child to think about and that was a lot more important than my pride.

"Three months after our daughter, Caroline, was born he came home late for dinner. He'd been at work all day and then had stopped by a bar near the office. I could smell the liquor as soon as he stepped into the kitchen. His face was flushed and he looked really ugly. This time I could feel it coming. Just as he got into the kitchen the baby started crying in the second bedroom. I made to go for her but he grabbed both my arms and said, 'I'll get her.' I was frightened for her and tried to push past him and with that he shoved me back against the refrigerator. This time he really beat me up."

Involuntarily, her hand strayed to her jaw and moved across her face. "I started to vomit blood. Maybe that scared him, I don't know, but I crawled across the floor to the bathroom and stayed there. By now the baby was screaming and I was terrified he'd go after her. So I got myself on my feet and I armed myself with a can of insect spray that was under the sink. I'd seen Farrah Fawcett do that in a movie in which she was raped and it blinded the guy, at least for a while. So I held that in my hand and draped a towel over my arm and came out and went to the baby's room.

"He didn't stop me. He was sitting on the couch pouring himself a drink and he didn't even look at me. I picked the baby up. She was cold and soaked and hungry but I knew she would survive and I wasn't sure I would. I took her into the bedroom, turned the bedside radio on real loud, and phoned the police.

"They were at the door in about seven minutes. I charged him with assault — domestic violence. I couldn't believe myself as I did it. Joe didn't say a word, he just looked at me: it was hard to tell if he knew what was going on. I hadn't planned on getting the police but suddenly I was deadly calm and was sure it was the right thing to do. Joe had to get help, I had to get help, and there wasn't any help outside. But he'd get it inside, of that I was sure."

With sharp, precise gestures she stubbed out her cigarette.

"I was very naive. I had a lot of faith in the system. The system is there and it's supposed to work for you. So I did what had to be done. Today, I understand better why women don't charge their husbands. I did a victim impact report and I said *this* wasn't my husband Joe, that he wasn't a criminal, that he held down a good job and had a family, and what he needed was help.

"What he got was three years. I got a surprise myself. It

turned out he had a provincial record of assault — on his first wife. He'd told me they'd been divorced because she had become involved with someone else. I'm glad I found out that he'd lied to me because we were really able to have it out while he was out on bail. Once a man's in prison there's no arguing or fighting or clearing things up with your partner. You're watched by prison staff the whole time and if you start fighting or even raising your voice in the visiting area the guard will tell you to leave, and it's all noted down and goes against any chance of parole.

"Anyway, I phoned mum and dad — from hospital — the night Joe was arrested and I told them everything. I had to, because I'd taken Caroline with me to Emergency, but the doctor there insisted that I stay at least overnight so I needed them to take the baby. I had a couple of broken ribs, a cut over my eye that needed stitching, and a lot of bruising.

"When they saw me mum started crying. They wanted me to go back home till I got on my feet but I didn't want to. I was in a state of shock but deep down I felt strong. I'm a domestic type but I'm not dependent or helpless. I'm no masochist either. Most women who get beaten feel they deserve it. I didn't. On the other hand I wasn't going to throw my marriage away like that." She tossed out a hand. "I wanted at least a chance to work it out — but between *us*, for *us* to do it. I felt if we were going to make it we'd have to make it by ourselves, that if I leaned on my parents it would cut down on the chances. Dad would have been glad to see Joe go to prison for life.

"Anyway, Joe spent the first year in Collins Bay and right up to the time of his parole eligibility date, he got no help at all. Then of course he didn't get a parole because he hadn't been treated! That system is really something! Every day I woke up and cursed myself for having put him there.

"Then he was transferred to Warkworth and they have a psychologist there and after three months on the waiting-list he got in to see him. Now he sees him for half an hour every two weeks: he'd like to go once a week but he's lucky to see him at all. It's helping him, and it's helping me too, because, like I said, not a day went by of that first year when I didn't bitterly resent him being in there and kick myself for my naiveté in sending him there."

I asked Sharon how things were now between her and Joe. She took her time in answering, then said slowly, "They aren't bad. In fact, they are probably better than they've ever been, even though I don't feel so great about it. Better, because now things are out in the open with us — why he lied to me about his first marriage, why he felt he had the right to beat me." Sharon gave a wry smile. "He even told me he didn't beat me because he was drunk, but that he'd actually start drinking so he could beat me.

"But it's really shitty all around having a man in prison. When he was in Collins Bay I moved to Kingston and visited at every opportunity. We'd had a lovely apartment in Toronto — well, at least compared to what I could afford in Kingston. But I figured that in six months our savings would run out and I'd have to go on welfare. I didn't have any job training and I had the baby anyway. So I got a small place just a bit out of Kingston and made do as best I could.

"God, was I ever lonely in that rat-hole of a place! Nobody stood by me. I didn't know anyone in town and if you're a stranger in a place like Kingston with a baby, no money, and no man, you might as well be branded with an I.W. on your fore-head — Inmate's Wife."

She opened a desk drawer, pulled out a tissue, and vigorously blew her nose before continuing.

"Mum and dad tried to help, but the whole situation caused them so much stress I asked them to stay away. Diane tried, too, but she couldn't stop telling me to get out of it. And not one of my girlfriends, not one, understood that I had a real commit-ment to try and make my marriage work. Do you know what it's like to visit in prison? It's got to be one of the most demeaning things that can happen to you. You get a feeling — when you hand your bag over or go through the barriers or when you line up with all the other women who are waiting with their kids outside the gate — you feel *you* are part of the prison system, like there's something the matter with *you*, like you're guilty too."

The worst part, said Sharon, was the crowding in the visiting area, making it impossible to have a private conversation.

"There are days when I just want to go in there and dump! I want to tell Joe how lousy the apartment is, and how worried I am about money, and that the baby has been crying half the night, and how goddamned lonely I am, and I want to scream at him that it's all his damned fault! But you can't. They're the ones in prison and you're supposed to be the one that's free and okay, and if you dump like that and they get depressed, it will all go against you. Because you're there to be cheering them up!

"Eventually I moved back to Toronto. I did a lot of thinking; you might say I did a lot of growing up. When Joe started with the psychologist, and at last got some of the help I'd turned him in for, I moved in with my parents in Brampton. Pride's okay but it was just breaking all of us up. Mum and dad really wanted to help and I was just hurting them by rejecting it. I realized everyone had been hurt by what Joe did: he wasn't the only one I had to consider.

"My parents lent me their car and I limited my visiting to Warkworth to weekends. I met another wife there with a two-year-old and we got on real good. She wanted to go back to school, too, so we got an apartment. We're both on welfare, but my parents help out on the side."

I asked Sharon just how optimistic was she that things would work out with Joe. She said she didn't know.

"Let's just say I'd like my daughter to have her own real father. I would like my marriage to work. We're the only family he's got. He's no fool and he's gaining a lot of self-understanding from the psychologist, as well as from the books he's been given to read."

A few minutes later she said, "You're wondering whether I think it's been worth it — the marriage, the whole bit. I can't answer that — yet. But I can tell you one thing: there's not one reason in the world to have Joe in prison. He'd learned his lesson the day he was arrested, when he'd sobered up and found himself in that stinking jail. Any alternative, if he got the help he needed, would have been better — and a damn sight less costly to everyone — than putting him in prison."

Gail Lawson lived in a North Vancouver apartment, a tastefully decorated two-bedroom unit near the water, with a splendid view of the harbour and the city. She was thirty-four, the owner of a small gift shop in one of the north shore's shopping-centres. It was a business she had started with a minimum of capital after her husband, Laurie, was sentenced to nine years for armed robbery of a bank on South Granville Street, Vancouver. During the robbery a bystander was wounded by a shot fired by Lawson's partner, Bob Stetson, who got fifteen years. Lawson, who was unarmed, drew a lighter sentence. It was Lawson's second conviction, and there was a gap of twelve years between this and his previous offence, also for armed robbery.

"The system sucks," said Gail. "Once you get into it there doesn't seem to be any way out, at least that's the way I feel now."

Lawson, just completing four and a half years of his time, had turned police informer. Through a fellow prisoner, since transferred to Millhaven, Ontario, Lawson had learned the identity of a long-sought killer of a southern Ontario RCMP officer. Through a series of secretly arranged interviews, which resulted in Lawson being placed in administrative segregation and being visited by a plainclothes Mountie, Lawson passed the critical information on to the RCMP.

At this time Lawson's mandatory supervision date was only eighteen months off, time which Lawson could have handled without much difficulty. However, Lawson claimed that he had totally changed, that he had made up his mind to go straight for the rest of his life. The reason? "I'm thirty-eight, I haven't made a dime from crime, and yet I've spent a fifth of my life in prison."

Lawson offered this information to the authorities as proof that he wished to dissociate himself forever from crime. It was accepted as such. The Mounties in return promised Lawson that on his release they would relocate him and his wife — they had no children — in a remote northern B.C. town, and would set them up with completely new identities.

Lawson had passed his parole eligibility date eighteen months earlier. Despite consistently good behaviour and no institutional charges, he had not been granted parole because of the grave nature of the offence.

Lawson's life inside any institution was now in grave danger. "Ratting" on another inmate is a fundamental breach of the inmate code and usually results in the informer being severely beaten or knifed. When an inmate rats in the death of a police officer, however, his life isn't worth a cent. No matter what precautions prison officials have taken to protect the prisoner, the truth is often on the inmate grapevine within a matter of hours.

Nor is the inmate safe once he hits the streets. His only chance of survival is to assume a new identity and cut off all criminal contacts from his past. Because of the risk he is taking, an inmate who rats is usually believed when he claims he wants to dissociate himself from his past. Lawson was now scheduled for another parole hearing, and there was little doubt that parole would be granted.

This was the day that Gail had longed for through five years of visiting the prison. (Lawson was remanded to prison for six months before and during his trial.) Now that the parole date was approaching she was filled with anger, frustration, and uncertainty. Pouring out two mugs of coffee from the steel pot that stood on the glass coffee-table, she made herself comfortable on the couch and idly chatted about the weather until I asked her how she'd met Laurie.

"I was friends with Laurie's sister, Anne. Anne and I once worked together in the office of a wholesale importer. After we'd both left we stayed in touch and about once a month we'd go bowling together. I never knew she had a brother until she introduced me to Laurie.

"Laurie and I hit it off from the start. He was, let's see, I was twenty-three so he was twenty-nine. There was a lot of chemistry involved, but it was more than that. For me, he was the one. And he felt the same about me. Anyway, we decided to move in together: in fact, it's still common law, our relationship."

Did Gail know by then that Laurie had a record?

"Yes," she said. "I was sort of beginning to think there'd been something, that maybe he'd been ill, or — you'll laugh at this — maybe he'd been in some sort of secret service or something, or was an undercover cop. He was really physically fit, and kind of sophisticated and cool. I remember asking him a while after we'd met where he'd gone for his vacation the year before. And he paused. You know that kind of a pause? Maybe just a second too long, but you know the other person is not being straight. When I asked him where he worked — he was a welder and had his papers — he said he was in the middle of changing jobs. And I remember Anne looked a bit funny when I asked her where she'd been keeping her brother, and she said something like, why don't you ask him?

"After we'd been going together for a few weeks Laurie told me he'd done time for a bank robbery and he'd just gotten out. I almost died. I'd never met anyone who'd been in prison before. I think it made him a bit more attractive to me. On the other hand it bothered me a bit, but I didn't think too much about it as I didn't want anything messing up our relationship. And I felt he was making a new beginning, he'd paid his debt, and it was in the past. I felt I could help him. I felt challenged, and I like to be challenged."

Three years passed. Gail said she and Laurie made a "fantastic" couple. "We were really happy," she said. "We seemed to have it made. The only thing we ever quarrelled about was money. I wanted to save and Laurie liked spending. I'd always wanted to have a small, elegant gift shop. I'd worked with a couple of wholesale importers and I had the contacts, but I needed money. So I saved everything I could. . . . But Laurie's no saver and he'd spend everything he could." Gail paused and swept her hand around the room: "All this furniture, all expensive stuff, it was Laurie who insisted we buy it. I must say it's been nice to have, though, during these years.

"Anyway, just about the same time I was thinking we had enough to get a small business going, the company Laurie worked for lost a big contract and he lost his job.

"About this time he also ran into an old buddy who was an ex-inmate, or at least that's what he later told me. I didn't like him seeing anyone who'd done time. Laurie's weak: he likes people to like him. He hates to say no to anybody, even if it's harmful to himself. I told him he was never to bring one of them home, but now I know he kept in touch with Bob Stetson and saw him from time to time.

"I was sitting at work one day, thinking that soon I'd be able to give notice and start my own shop, when I saw the blue and white of an RCMP car pull up in front. I just knew as soon as I saw them walk towards the store that they were coming to me. Laurie had been arrested three hours earlier. He and Bob only got four blocks from the bank before they were picked up."

Gail's voice was flat and tinged with bitterness.

"He was held in the remand centre downtown for the preliminary and then went to Oakalla. I went to see him only a couple of times, I felt that bitter. Both times I went I cried so much it didn't do him any good and it didn't do me any good. I got a good lawyer for him. Laurie decided to plead guilty, but he still got nine years and I still lost half my savings.

"I quit my job: the publicity drove me out. There wasn't much of a story in the paper but it doesn't take much. Everyone in the store knew. I'd always handled the cash in my department. After Laurie's arrest I felt I wasn't trusted anymore. It was probably all in my head, but it became harder and harder. If I 'd immediately cut off all contact with him, and said I was leaving him, I'd have been all right at work. But I didn't, and there was so much embarrassment and strain that after a few weeks I left. People out there still feel women gain their identity from their partner."

Gail's eyes filled with tears. "I loved the guy so much. We really were close. I felt he was my best friend . . . and he did this to me! I mean, he wasn't the only one that got time. I got it too. Every day for nearly five years I've served my time too. For four months I didn't go see him. I felt too weepy, too hurt, too angry. I felt he'd taken my life away from me. Sometimes I felt if I got close to him I'd kill him. So I stayed away until I felt I could handle it, but when I got there I couldn't. I cried so much and it upset him so much, the authorities told me I couldn't come back for a month."

Gail gradually got her life back together. "My family — that's my parents and my brother, Chris — were terrific. And Anne was as good as any sister could have been, although she also had to cope with her parents. They're an old couple in their seventies, and God knows they'd been through enough when Laurie went to prison the first time."

Gail decided to make as much money as she could while Laurie was imprisoned. "I was very lucky. Through a friend of Anne's I got on as a waitress at the Hotel Granville on Granville Island. I worked the night shift and did really well with tips. Then three days a week I worked at Eaton's in sales. I was familiar with the computerized sales registry and during the busy seasons they wanted me in all the time. I felt half dead I was so tired, but I stuck with it.

"On Sundays I went to see Laurie. It was my entire social life, visiting in prison. For the first few months we hashed and rehashed the reasons why he'd gotten into this mess. He tried to manipulate me, like hinting he'd done it for me, to get money for me and my shop. He made out almost as if I was responsible! But there was no way I'd let him get away with that. I felt we had to lay it all out so we could avoid it ever happening again. There was no one to help me through this time, no one to help him. I mean, Laurie didn't have an alcohol problem, he didn't do drugs, he didn't have an uncontrollable temper, he wasn't sexually sick. He was weak and greedy. There just weren't any programs for him to get into and there certainly wasn't any supportive system for me. In fact, I had no one from the prison system to speak to, no one that I could open up to, let alone someone who knew how to help me.

"God, it was a hideous time! There's no privacy in the visiting area. Kids are everywhere. At times the tension's so thick you could cut it. You don't want to start off with touchy subjects so you leave them towards the end and then there's an argument, and it's time up, and you have to split with both of you feeling terrible. There's no closeness allowed. A kiss when you come, a kiss when you go. After the first few months you've talked about everything. Life's so different inside prison, so isolated, so controlled, there's not all that much to talk about.

"To be honest, after I got used to Laurie not being with me I got a lot of satisfaction out of saving and moving towards my goal, and finally getting my own business. I could sense that Laurie was only so-so interested. I can't say he resented it, he was happy for me, but he really didn't want to hear much about it. So you start to fantasize together about the future, how it's going to be when he gets out. And it was okay if I talked about the business in that sense, both of us sharing it, and maybe buying a house, and a new car.

"But now because of him talking to the Mounties we've got to go live in some to-hell-and-gone place, and I've got to give it all up, everything, everything I've worked for, all the goodwill I've built up, all the suppliers I know, all the customers who like me. . . . " Her voice trailed off.

"I've asked myself if I wish he hadn't passed that name on to the police. It would have made everything easier. But in the end I'm glad he did. He doesn't have any options now but to go straight. It makes me feel surer of him, closer to him. And that cop's widow. I imagine it means a lot to her to know they caught her husband's killer."

Mandy Morrison had lived with Ron Parker for three years when he was sentenced to three years for possession of stolen goods, and one year concurrent for possession of an unregistered weapon. Parker, twenty-four, had had two previous convictions for possession, but this was his first federal time.

Morrison, twenty-two, had two small children by a previous relationship, and a baby by Parker at the time he was sentenced. Her mother and stepfather cared full-time for the two older children, leaving Morrison with responsibility only for the baby.

"When I was a kid, my dad went to prison. I don't know what it was for or whether it was a provincial or federal one, but I remember being taken there by mum, and I remember seeing my dad there and the funny way it smelled, like antiseptic mixed with grease.

"The kids at school knew my dad was in jail, they used to tease me about it. I asked mum once why he was there but she never did tell me, just got really mad. I remember once going to a neighbour's to play and the woman taking her kids in, saying she didn't want them playing with 'jailbird kids'.

"I told Ron from the start that if he messed around with crime I'd leave him. He'd threaten me when I said that, but my kids weren't going to go through what I went through. I remember mum and I, we were always poor. Mum used to clean houses for money, and then she'd take me to St. Vinney's — you know, the St. Vincent's shop with old clothes and things — and she'd pick my dresses out of a barrel.

"She didn't like it much when I started hanging out with Ron and she found out he had a record. She said she knew by looking at him, that he had a look about him! It didn't stop me, though. We moved in together and everything was okay until the cops came one day to the house and tramped through it, turning everything upside down and pulling out all the drawers and wrecking the place, like a bunch of effing thugs. I knew Ron was involved in something. I'd suspected it because he'd gotten these funny phone calls, and guys came around I'd never seen before. When I asked him what was going on, he told me to butt out.

"The cops picked him up, just in front of our house, with everyone down the street watching. You've got to have it happen to you to know what it feels like. I felt I was dying of shame, all the feelings about mum and me alone came back, all the feelings I had as a kid about dad being in prison — it all came back.

"After he was sentenced I went to see him once. I wanted to make sure he wasn't waiting for me, like I used to wait for dad, it seemed forever. I told him it was over, he could screw up his life, but he wasn't going to screw up mine and my kids' as well. He got mad and called me names, quietly, the way you have to in prison, and then he started crying. His temper was okay, I could deal with that. But his crying made me sick. It reminded me of dad, snivelling in the same way years earlier, trying to make mum feel sorry for him, setting her up so she'd stick with him.

"That was nine months ago and I guess he'll be getting out in a few months, but I don't want him back. I won't go through any of that stuff, never, for nobody. I've gotten by on welfare. No man's worth that — all you go through, being searched, feeling like you was a criminal too, having the cops go through your house like you didn't exist.

"You may be wondering if I loved Ron. Well I did, but since I was a kid I've tried to make myself feel good about myself. You know what I mean? Give myself some confidence. And how can I do that if I get sucked up into the whole prison bit? You know, all that goes along with the visiting, the way some of the screws look at you, the way people stare when they find out your man's doing time. If I went along with that, couldn't a person, knowing about my dad, couldn't they say about me, 'Hasn't she learned anything in life?'"

Betty Louis was twenty-seven when her husband, Ken, also twenty-seven, was sentenced to life for first-degree murder — a sentence of twenty-five years without parole. Their children were aged two, five, and seven.

Ken, a heavy drinker, shot another man in a drunken brawl. Betty maintained that if they could have afforded a good lawyer Ken would have got off with manslaughter. She was probably right. I've seen many cases where the killings were more deliberate and premeditated, plea bargaining has reduced the charge to manslaughter, and the penalty has been three years.

Betty was now thirty-two. Her children, now seven, ten, and twelve, hated to visit prison. They barely remembered their father and they resented his attempts to assume a paternal, disciplinary role. Betty felt the time had come to leave them at home, to let them forget their father, but Ken desperately needed to keep in touch with his children.

"I can understand why Ken wants to see them at every chance, but I don't like my kids being in prison once or twice a week. They know it's a prison. How much of it are they soaking up? I'm scared stiff they'll get used to it, that they'll go that way when they're teenagers. It's always at the back of my mind, that they'll end up in a place like that. It makes me awfully hard on them. We'll both be fifty-two when he gets out. Our children will be long grown up. Most of my life will be over.

"At first, Ken didn't want me to visit, he said I was free to go, he told me to get a divorce. The first time I was allowed to visit he refused to see me. It just about killed me. No one encouraged me to stay with him — not my parents or anyone else. There was no one for me to really talk to about what was happening to me, or to him, or how the system worked. I knew the children would suffer if I stayed, I mean, not only don't they have no father, there's not much of anything else. I had to go on welfare right away, and by the time I pay all my expenses, there's hardly anything left for food.

"But he's my husband. His whole family's up north. No one else goes visit him. I'm all he's got, me and the kids. He needs me. Someone's got to give him support.

"I think Ken should pay for what he did. I know the victim left a widow and a child and he can never make up for that. But sometimes I think I'm worse off than she is. I'm not a widow, but I don't feel either married or unmarried. I can't have any social life because I'm married and if I go anywhere alone . . . well, men are aware of you and that's asking for trouble. But I don't have a husband — no one to help with the kids, or with money, or around the house or yard. But *I* didn't commit any crime, *I* didn't do anything." Betty's voice betrayed her anger.

"The way I feel is that he's done five years and I've done five years, and the kids in their way have done five years. All the system is doing from now on is damaging him. Is he really going to be a better man after twenty more years? Who's kidding who? All he'll be is an old man, bitter and unable to function."

Mothers who wait usually don't have to worry about rent, the phone, the electricity bill, and being able to eat, as younger women do. They are not deprived of a sexual life, nor of the companionship of their spouse. They are not the odd women out in social gatherings, nor are they confused by the necessity of playing a phony maternal role to the inmate. But the suffering of mothers who wait has its own character. They often feel shattering guilt, deep depression, and a profound sense of failure as women and mothers.

Rose Smith, fifty-four, worked in Winnipeg as a waitress, her lifelong occupation. She and her husband were divorced when their son, Rory, was aged four.

"I never had any money. I used to leave Rory with this old lady downstairs for two dollars a day. She was well-meaning but muddled. I lived almost downtown, close to work to save the bus fares. There weren't any nurseries downtown and I couldn't have afforded one if there were. Rory hated going to the old lady: he used to scream when I'd leave him off. Sometimes he'd have an ear-ache. He didn't get the care a kid should have. But I did my best. Later when he started school he got a lot of colds and sometimes would be quite sick. But I'd make him go: I was frightened of leaving him alone in the flat all day, like you know the things kids can do with matches, or maybe some queer would come around. Anyway, I'd make him go, sick or not, I felt I had no choice. Once the school nurse rang me up at work and told me to pick him up and take him home to bed. I did but I nearly lost my job. I was so ashamed."

Rose said she spoiled Rory because she felt guilty, letting him have his own way until, as an unsupervised teenager, he was out of control. By the time he was seventeen he had a juvenile record for drug use, and break-and-enter, and by the time he was nineteen he was in a federal penitentiary.

"I've never had any bad experiences coming and going in the prison," she said. "The guards always treat me right; maybe it's my grey hair. They sometimes have a smile and say good evening: it depends on who's on. But I feel such guilt, such shame, in front of them. My girlfriends, they know Rory's here, and they're sorry for me, but they never mention him. They talk about their own kids but never ask after him. I understand but it hurts.

"The only time I feel all right is when I'm actually with Rory, and I can be a mother to him. The rest of the time I feel like I'm crying inside. He's coming out soon and he's coming home. I'm what they call his 'community support'.

"The only person I've been able to talk to has been my doctor. I told him it was like Rory was dead, the feeling I've got of mourning and grieving. He said I've got to get help. But there isn't any help to get. There's none for Rory inside and none for me outside."

I have interviewed over fifty women with loved ones in prison, and every one felt strongly that her own suffering would be worthwhile if there were solid rehabilitation programs available to her man in prison, programs that would give the inmate trade skills to make a living, and personal skills necessary for a stable, law-abiding life.

Not only the inmate needs help to understand his behaviour and training to make positive rather than destructive choices. Those who will live with him — those the system depends on to help keep him straight — are, sometimes desperately, in need of supportive programs themselves. Experienced parole officers know that there is a strong correlation between solid family support and parole success. Until recently, the family's existence was not even recognized until the inmate was near release. Now a community assessment is done with the family immediately after the inmate has been sentenced. If families who are helping an inmate return to society are helped themselves, the chances of a parolee's success are increased.

Many of the women involved with inmates have little idea how the criminal justice system works, nor do they understand the underlying factors that contribute to criminal or addictive behaviour. They may come from emotionally deprived backgrounds and lack education. Nevertheless, they are expected to deal with some of the most difficult men in the community, men who are sometimes embittered, often manipulative, men with short fuses and violent tempers, men who often have few social skills, or an addiction problem, men who gain their own way by threats and intimidation.

Programs that systematically address the needs of inmates' families are a necessity if the criminal justice system and the community are serious in their expressed desire to reduce recidivism, or relapses into crime. These programs could be created and run in a number of ways — through the government; through non-profit societies that already work in corrections, such as the John Howard Society or the Elizabeth Fry Society; or through qualified private volunteers. They should start in the prison and continue in the community.

The task of building relationships, of creating love and trust, of maintaining old links and building new ones, and of healing and making whole, has usually been women's work. The introduction of family-therapy programs would acknowledge this potential strength and could signal the beginning of a true commitment to rehabilitation.

7   *Yesterday's Failed Children*

One only has to work in any prison for a few days to realize that prisons are institutions primarily for the poor. They are the bottom rung of the welfare system, one rung lower than the regular welfare system, where society's greatest failures are kept out of public view and these failed children are fed, clothed, and sheltered.

This is not to say that many poor people are criminals, or that well-to-do people are all law-abiding, nor to deny that the criminal has free will. It is simply to say that most criminals *who are caught and incarcerated* are the products of poverty. White-collar crime is difficult to prove and you don't find well-educated or middle-class people in the lockup for holding up a 7-Eleven store with a penknife, doing a series of neighbourhood break-and-enters, or clobbering a cab driver for his money. The well-off already have the things that can be obtained from this type of crime. When they are incarcerated it's for cooking a company's books and creaming off someone's estate, or killing a spouse or lover who has become a nuisance, or becoming involved in some grandiose scheme to bring in a yachtful of drugs.

Of the majority of prison poor, some have extremely high IQs (120 and over) and some are in the slow-to-defective range (below 80). Reliable statistics on literacy, or on any number of subjects relating to prison and prisoners, are virtually impossible to obtain. For example, according to the *Southam Report on*

Illiteracy, released March 4, 1987, 24 percent of the general population have less than a grade nine education and are therefore categorized as functionally illiterate, while 50 percent of Canada's prison population have less than grade nine. Of the six thousand inmates who are categorized as functionally illiterate, the *Southam Report* states that only five hundred are taking upgrading courses. But according to Correctional Service Canada's in-house publication, *Let's Talk* (Volume 10, No. 2, January 30, 1985) only 6 percent of the general population and 18 percent of the federal prison population are considered functionally illiterate. In this study functional illiteracy was taken to apply to those who had less than grade five education.

It is plainly evident to anyone working with prisoners that the majority of inmates are, in varying degrees, handicapped by their lack of reading and writing skills. Some suffer from untreated learning disabilities that have been diagnosed only since incarceration, others have physical disabilities that have prevented learning, such as poor eyesight or limited hearing.

Whether inmates rate high or low on intelligence tests makes little difference to their overall psychological profile. They are often inarticulate, confused, and emotionally immature; they have little if any sense of identity, are dependent on everyone but themselves, handle normal pressures badly and may resort to alcohol and/or drugs to cope. As a group they have chips on their shoulders: they feel the world owes them. They are yesterday's abused children.

The extent of child abuse and extreme emotional deprivation in the formative years of many inmates is so striking that when I first started studying the dossiers I wondered if I'd gotten hold of a control group, or an unusual group of particularly maltreated children, now incarcerated adults, who were under study.

As a reporter I'd never thought of myself as naive. From the mid 1950s to the mid 1970s there was a lot written about child abuse and I wrote my share of it. But when I came at the problem as a reporter, it was from the top looking down. Other middle-class professionals and I examined this terrible problem from a distance. We knew it was widespread, and not confined to any particular class or socio-economic group, but we still regarded it as exceptional.

In prisons I found a sub-stratum of society where abuse is the normal pattern of childhood, and a stable, loving, nurturing beginning the exception. When I came face to face with this "shadow world" of unpredictable parental reaction, strappings, hunger, isolation, abandonment, rejection, alcoholism, body blows, sexual assault, and various forms of torture and dehumanization, I felt outraged. It was clear that the crimes these men had been incarcerated for were often less serious than those committed against them.

For three years I kept a tally of the family and social history of all inmates between the ages of eighteen and forty whom I interviewed. Seventy-eight percent had been cruelly abused as children. This doesn't mean that these inmates were safe to release or that society owed them a release, even though it was society's indifference to ensuring adequate child care for them that was partly responsible for the abuse in the first place. Some were as dangerous as mad dogs with their pain, others had had the stuffing knocked out of them and could barely function. All were fearful and unable to trust anyone.

Francis Roberts was nineteen when he applied for full parole and came up for a hearing at Bowden medium-security institution, a couple of hours' drive north of Calgary. He was a sad-faced kid, long and thin, with straight, fair hair down to his shoulders.

Roberts was serving two years on two counts of break-and-enter and theft; possession of a weapon dangerous to the public peace; and failure to appear before the court. The first charge involved breaking into two shops and stealing a Sony radio from one and cassettes from the other. The weapon charge resulted from an argument with a friend during which Roberts had pulled out an imitation switch-blade knife and threatened his friend. These weren't his first charges. He had committed several thefts and had one charge of possession of stolen property on his record. As a result of several minor offences he had been in jail more or less since he was sixteen.

We saw him in February. He had been seen earlier for parole but had been denied. His mandatory supervision date was in July, only five months away. If Roberts wasn't simply going to be dumped onto the street at his MS date, the parole service had to come up with some sort of viable release program for him now. This would establish some badly needed outside support for him following his release and set up some control over his whereabouts and activities.

Roberts had two institutional charges. One was for having paint thinner in his possession; he'd spent five days locked up in his cell for that. The other was for having "brew" (illicit home-made liquor) in his possession, for which he'd spent fifteen days in the hole. Both these charges indicated substance dependency, although his record showed no history of such a problem.

As soon as I met Roberts, I knew why he'd been denied parole. He was a psychological mess, a bag of pain. There was nothing wrong with his brains: he'd completed grade ten in the institution and had done some work in automotive mechanics.

Roberts did not know where he was born or who his parents were, or what his real name was. At the age of three he was spotted by a railway guard, standing alone on a deserted railway platform in southern Saskatchewan. He was well dressed, with a tweed overcoat, a matching cap on his head, and a dime in his hand. The name of the railway station was pinned to his coat.

The guard, knowing no other trains were passing through and confident the child's relatives would arrive at any moment, left him there. When he returned that night, the boy was still there, curled up on the platform asleep. The guard contacted the RCMP and that was the beginning of Roberts's file.

All efforts to trace his parents failed. A guard on the train that brought the child admitted lifting him aboard, and accepting ten dollars from a pretty woman who asked him to put the child out at his destination, where relatives would be waiting. The story was a hoax: no relatives ever came forward to claim the child.

Roberts was held in a children's agency home, along with other abandoned and displaced children, and some months later was placed in a foster home. He was there for three years and did well. Just as he was about to start school, his foster father was killed in a traffic accident and the boy was returned to the agency home. His placements after that became increasingly frequent as his behaviour required more and more skill to handle. He did not act out: he was not aggressive. He simply stopped talking. His grades fell: he hated school and refused to go. It became impossible to get him to do anything. All he wanted to do was sit and stare. He didn't know what the problem was and, apparently, neither did anyone else.

At the age of ten he was placed in a permanent foster home, a farm some miles out of the nearest town which had taken on various foster children over the years and used them as cheap labour. There he was subject to severe beatings by his foster father. On one occasion the man picked him up and slammed his head against a cement wall. He ran away at fifteen, worked as a casual farm labourer for one season, and was in jail for break-and-enter before the year was up. Since then he had more or less remained in jail.

At Bowden prison in Alberta, where we were now seeing him, he functioned quite well. Bowden is one of the better institutions as far as staff-inmate relations are concerned and Roberts had responded to the efforts of staff to get him to accept some responsibility for his own future. He got himself a job in the kitchen, where he was known as a slow but reliable worker.

The board was now looking at a nineteen-year-old with a growing criminal record, but one who was not really "criminalized". That became evident as we talked to him. He wanted "to work and earn some money," he said. He wanted to "save some of his money and buy a house." He wanted to have a girlfriend, and maybe later get married. There wasn't a trace of a punk mentality about him.

The police report of his apprehension and arrest supported our assessment. Police reports are often curiously sympathetic, particularly in the small towns and rural areas. "Basically not the criminal type," it said. "Offered no resistance and was completely co-operative. Admitted all his offences and saved us a lot of work. A lad who would benefit greatly by some firm guidance."

Whatever Roberts's potential, his longing for a "normal" life was, at this stage, the stuff of dreams. The reality was that he had neither work skills nor social skills. He had never had one continuing human contact in his life, not one person over the years who cared whether he lived or died. He didn't know whether his mother had abandoned him with tears or with relief. He didn't know if he looked like his father, whether his grandparents were still alive, or whether he had brothers or sisters. He didn't know if he was part Norwegian, French, German, or Swedish. He didn't know if he was supposed to be a Catholic or a Mennonite or a Baptist. Every time he looked inside himself it must have been like falling off a cliff.

"Frank," I said, after asking permission to use his first name, "tell us about these charges on your sheet — the paint thinner and brew in your possession. Have you been sniffing?"

"A bit," he said quietly.

"You know it will fry your brains," I said. "You must be feeling pretty bad to do something like that to yourself. Are you worried about going outside? Or is this place getting to you?"

"I'm just existing right now," he said. "It'll be better when I'm on the outside." There was a long pause. "When I get out, I'll be able to make some money, get a job. . . ." His voice faded.

"Frank, it was hard for you to find work before and not having a job, among other things, has gotten you into trouble." I checked through the police report. "I see here that in some of the break-and-enters you were stealing food and clothes."

"I needed things," he said. "It was winter, I didn't have a jacket. And I hadn't eaten."

"What about the radio? What about the cassettes?"

There was a long pause. He said nothing. I let it pass. He would have sold both goods on the street for a few dollars — maybe to some "honest" citizen who closed his mind to the possibility they were hot.

"Frank, you know you really don't have any marketable job skills. You've got a growing criminal record that directly relates to that fact. I see that you've asked for a parole to go to Grierson Centre in Edmonton, with the hope of getting involved in the workers' program there. But your parole officer believes it's more important for you to do the life-skills program there, and so do we."

"I've gotta get some money. I don't have anything. Nothing."

"That's why it's important for you to do the life-skills course. It will teach you how to apply for a job, how to present yourself, how to hold a job. It will show you a lot that will be helpful." There was no response. "Frank, we'd like to move you out of here and get you settled on the outside before your MS date, but there's no point in us doing that if you don't take life-skills."

Roberts had already done a full year in prison, which meant that for a full year a professional therapist could have been working with him to help him gain some internal controls. Even a skilled counsellor could have reached this wounded kid and have given him some understanding of what made him tick and what a dangerous route he was beginning to take. But there was no professional help available. The staff had done what they could, but it wasn't their job, nor did they have the time, to give Roberts what he needed.

He had been assessed once by an outside psychiatrist who told us what we could already observe: "This fellow is not criminally oriented but is the simple product of misfortune. He has been knocked around a lot and needs a lot of guidance. He is very needy at all levels. He will need consistent care if this neediness is not to lead him into unacceptable or illegal behaviour."

Consistent care! There was no way that a six-week life-skills course with a group of other inmates after a lifetime of deprivation could provide "consistent care". But what else was there? This was just another case where a little something was better than an absolute nothing.

Roberts was granted his parole to Grierson Centre with the stipulation that he complete the life-skills course and a request to staff that every effort be made to help him find employment. What he would do about the big black hole where his family memories, ego strengths, and identity should have been was not our problem — at least not this time around.

Jason Miles was the eldest of six children of an alcoholic father and an emotionally disturbed mother. He had been temporarily removed from his parents at the age of nine months following a violent beating of his mother that brought in the police. The intervening officers noted that the infant appeared severely undernourished, unable even to sit up by himself. He was taken and placed in the children's ward of the local hospital. He stayed there for three months, until he had gained normal weight and attained normal skills, then he was returned home.

The atmosphere in which Miles spent most of his formative years was one of quarrelling, severe beatings, days without food, explosions of anger, a filthy and chaotic house — and, when things got too bad, temporary removal to a foster home.

By the time he was eight, Miles had started drinking. At fourteen, after his father had used the buckle end of his belt on him and gashed his face, he left home, and he was on his own from then on. First he worked in a warehouse, and later with a moving company, but neither job lasted. Miles had grown into an immature, self-centred, moody adult, with a temper that was triggered by the slightest pressure. Fired from his job, Miles drifted across the country. He had done a fair bit of shoplifting as a child and easily graduated to break-and-enters. In fact, he *liked* to rip people off. It wasn't only the material rewards: he also got a deep pleasure from thieving, as if he were somehow squaring an account. He felt that anything he could get was owed to him.

Miles lived this way for four years, sharing a basement apartment with two other young men in Vancouver. He specialized in mid-afternoon B&Es, mainly in the high-rise apartments of the west end or in the old homes in the Kitsilano district that had been converted into smart townhouses.

One golden fall afternoon towards the end of October, 1982, Miles squeezed his way through a basement window of one of these townhouses. He had cased the place carefully, noting that there were no children and that husband and wife returned every day from work together at about 6 p.m.

As he reached the top of the stairs, a man wearing a dressing-gown and blowing his nose stepped out of the bedroom onto the landing. Seeing Miles, he froze in total astonishment.

Miles was less surprised. He had known that one day this would happen and he was prepared. From the back of his jeans he took out a spring-blade pocketknife.

"What the hell. . . . Get out of here!" the man yelled.

"Get back, get back!" Miles screamed. He struck the man full across the face with his fist and tried to tie him up as the man lay unconscious on the floor. But there was nothing suitable at hand except the cloth belt of the dressing-gown, and that was held down by the victim's body weight. Later, Miles told police, "I didn't mean to stab him. I panicked. He'd have been all right if I could have tied him up, but he kept breaking away."

Miles stabbed his victim twice in the back and once in the

chest. Minutes later he was still crouched on the floor at the side of the victim, kneeling, curled up, barely able to breathe. He described these moments to police as a struggle: although he did not want to hurt the man, he had the urge to go on stabbing.

After leaving the house, Miles put in an anonymous call to the police that an ambulance was needed at a given address. That action, and the skill of the cardiac unit at St. Paul's Hospital in treating the victim, saved him from a murder charge. One stab wound had penetrated the heart, a wound that a few years earlier would have led to the victim's death.

Two days later, Miles was picked up by a cruising police car whose officer recognized him from the composite drawing made up from the victim's description. He was charged and convicted of causing bodily harm with intent to wound, and break-and-enter, and was sentenced to four years and six months in February, 1983. That gave him a parole eligibility date of August, 1984, a mandatory supervision date of February, 1986, and a warrant expiry date of August, 1987.

We saw Miles — now a stocky, black-haired eighteen-year-old with a thick moustache — at Kent maximum-security prison in Agassiz, British Columbia. Because of the nature of his offence, his violent temper, and his inability to get along with others, he had originally been placed in Kent in an attempt to settle him down. At Kent there are no choices. It's a tightly run, electronically controlled cement and steel container with precise scheduling, limited intermingling of inmates, and one excellent if overworked psychologist.

On admission to Kent, Miles was in a deeply depressed, suicidal state. He was given a low doze of tranquillizer and seen by the psychologist twice. Gradually he stabilized and after nine months there without any institutional charges against him he was transferred to Matsqui medium-security institution. The lower the security of the institution, the better chance an inmate has for a conditional release.

Originally built as a drug-treatment centre, Matsqui has

always been an angry, simmering sort of place where there is more settling of scores, trading of drugs, and general wheeling and dealing than is possible at higher-security institutions such as Kent. (Older inmates often prefer the quiet and predictability of a highly restrictive maximum institution to the looser structures of the medium institutions, where "those noisy young punks are always in my hair," as one old-timer complained.)

Miles was at Matsqui three months when he became involved in settling a score for a buddy who had been "piped" (beaten with pipe or a baseball bat) by an "unknown assailant". All the inmates knew who had done the piping. Nobody talked but Miles acted impetuously. He confronted the assailant who sneered at him, calling him a "pint-sized bastard". He went berserk, grazed the cheekbone of his tormentor, and landed in the hole. From the hole he had been shipped back to Kent, where he had cooled his heels for four months. Now he was before us asking for parole.

Miles was entitled by law to a parole hearing. For the parole board members to make up their minds before the hearing started was contrary to our "duty to be fair". Yet there wasn't any chance that Miles was going to get anything from me or from anyone else on the board. Kent staff who had worked with Miles during his former stay had noted a deterioration in his attitude. He reacted to any control with open hostility. He refused to see the psychologist. He had become more rigid, more aggressive, less reachable. The starved and beaten baby Miles of eighteen years ago was now an unpredictable and violent adult, a potential danger to any community.

In cases like this I felt like a phony. Even though inmates had the right to refuse a hearing if they felt they had nothing to gain from it, some inmates assumed that the mere fact that the board had scheduled a hearing meant some hope. They ignored the fact that the board *had* to hold a hearing once eligibility had been reached and the inmate requested it.

The board denied Miles's parole, citing the violence of his

offence, the incident at Matsqui, and his recent lack of co-operation. But the underlying reason was his dangerous rage, spawned by the cruelty of his father and the inability of his mother to defend him and his siblings. Child welfare authorities who had repeatedly returned Miles to this violent and miserable home, out of some sentimental mission to "keep the family together" at any cost, shared some responsibility for the likelihood that Miles would probably spend most of his life in prison.

Mary Elizabeth Dennis was serving five years for killing her nine-month-old daughter, Chrystal. "A monstrous crime," the judge had told the weeping woman when he sentenced her. I met her in Fort Saskatchewan prison, to which she had been transferred after one year in the Kingston Prison for Women. Although she was a federal prisoner, Dennis had been moved to the provincial institution for "humanitarian reasons": her two surviving children were being looked after by her sister in nearby Saskatoon.

Dennis was one of five children who lived with their parents in a small town in northern Alberta. Her father was a rigid, severe man who had created a small but profitable business selling insurance. He was religious, an elder in one of the local churches, and a great believer in corporal punishment for small household infractions. Her mother spent her life cleaning the house and attempting to placate her husband.

When Dennis was nine her mother was hospitalized. She awoke in the middle of one night to find her father kneeling beside the bed feeling her body. She asked him to stop, and he did, saying that all he wanted to know was how "his little girl was growing." The following night Dennis was raped by her father and for the duration of the mother's hospitalization he continued to assault her.

In talking to a court-hired psychiatrist before her trial, Dennis described her memories of those times: "There was no lock on the bedroom door. My two young sisters, they had a bed in the room too. They'd be asleep before I went to bed. I used to lie there really scared that Dad would come in. I hated it. Sometimes I thought of running away, or getting a knife, or. . . . He'd talk like . . . about God . . . and how he was 'preparing me' to be a good wife . . . things like that, like he was being good to me. But I knew it was wrong. It hurt me and I felt dirty all over. He said if I told anyone he might end up going to jail and I'd be to blame. Like it'd be my fault for breaking up the family. I couldn't tell Mum. . . . I don't know why but I couldn't."

The abuse stopped when her mother returned from hospital but two years later it resumed and continued sporadically until Dennis had her first period. By then Dennis, an above-average student, hated school. "I felt there was something wrong with me. I felt different from the other girls. I felt the boys could tell. I hated getting undressed for gym. I felt everyone could tell about Dad and me just by looking at me."

Dennis started dating when she was fifteen. By the time she was sixteen she was pregnant and, at her parents' insistence, married. Her husband, Herbie, was a nineteen-year-old farm labourer from a large, impoverished family. With a flash of insight she told the psychiatrist: "I thought I loved him, but I guess all we both wanted was to get away from our parents."

The house in which the couple lived was described in the social worker's report as "adequate but more like a cabin or shack. Housekeeping standards were poor. Although there was running hot water there were dirty dishes in all four rooms. Washed but unironed clothes were scattered everywhere. The glass in the children's bedroom had been broken and taped over with newspaper. The curtains were torn and the linoleum split. Client told me the washing-machine had been broken for some months and clothes were dried on the line outside. There was no inside toilet. Furniture was adequate. Client seemed embarrassed by the conditions and overwhelmed by the demands on her."

This description was written some weeks before Dennis killed her baby. The social worker had visited the house following the hospitalization of the oldest child, three-year-old Jimmie, for a broken right arm. The worker reported that there was no indication of any child abuse and that, in fact, Dennis seemed concerned and affectionate towards the boy, her two-year-old daughter, Charlene, and baby Chrystal.

Dennis's husband, Herbie, showed more interest in drag-racing than he did in either his wife or family. When he was at home, the couple quarrelled continuously. Dennis had imagined her crippling guilt and shame would be washed away by being married and having her own children, but her self-loathing was getting worse. She hated herself, she hated Herbie, and there were times when she hated the children.

On the afternoon of the offence she was feeling particularly tense. The baby had cried on and off all night and Herbie had gone to work without speaking to her. She had asked him when he was going to fix the washing-machine and he had walked out, slamming the door. Dennis felt ill and exhausted, her period was late and she suspected that she was pregnant again.

Her one daily treat was the TV soap opera "The Young and the Restless". Shortly before its scheduled time she put the two older children in the backyard to play, but they kept toddling back into the house every few minutes. After a while she gave up and sat them on the floor with toys and Cheerios while she turned on the television. At that moment Jimmie hit Charlene and Charlene started to scream. The baby awoke and also started to howl. Dennis took the baby out of her crib, turned up the TV so she could hear it in the kitchen, warmed some milk, and returned to the living-room. As the two children continued to fight, Dennis could feel herself beginning to shake uncontrollably. Fearful that she might harm them, she picked up Jimmie and Charlene and shoved them out of doors, locking the kitchen door.

Baby Chrystal continued to scream. She twisted and turned her head whenever Dennis tried to give her the bottle. Finally, Dennis stood up and walked around with her, barely able to hear the TV above her screams. And then Dennis slapped the baby and the child screamed more. Dennis started shaking her, rattling her, until she couldn't stop. Next she knew the child was on the floor, blue-lipped and silent.

When we met Dennis she had served seventeen months of her five-year sentence — nearly one-third — and so was eligible for parole. A short woman in jeans, pale-faced and overweight, she obviously had taken care to present herself well for the hearing. Her fair hair fell straight to her shoulders, a little unkempt but clean, her nails had been manicured and painted pink, and she wore a string of imitation pearls at the neck of her sweater.

Dennis would never qualify as a potential "danger to society" in the same sense that a bank robber, fraud artist, or rapist would. Unless she received professional psychiatric counselling to help her overcome the damage done by both her incestuous father and her own criminal act — treatment that she had not yet received — the question of her "gaining maximum benefit from incarceration" was irrelevant. Dennis did not have antisocial, criminal attitudes that needed to be changed. Her father did, but he wasn't in prison: he was probably off somewhere holding church meetings.

In the hearing we concentrated on Dennis's surviving children, her plans to support herself, and the accommodation and community supports she would have available if allowed a release of some type. The older children had been removed from their father and placed in foster care immediately after the offence. In time Dennis's younger sister, Cheryl, only eighteen herself but married to a man in his twenties who was employed and stable, had convinced welfare authorities to give her and her husband custody of Jimmie and Charlene. Dennis said that she hoped to regain custody of her children one day. Our job was to satisfy ourselves that the release plan was suitable and that Dennis would present no danger to her children — or to any other children who might come into her life — if we released her.

This was not hard to do. Dennis had no record of petty theft, juvenile delinquency, alcoholism, drug use, or other violence. Physically exhausted and psychologically tormented, she had killed her child in a single outburst of aggression. It was a "situational" offence if ever there was one. She had been given five years by the court, but the same system that invested authority in the court to pass that sentence had invested authority in the board to grant a conditional release if she met certain conditions.

We were confident that she had met those conditions. As well, Dennis and her parole officer had worked out an excellent plan. The community assessment on her sister and her brother-in-law indicated that the house was large enough for all of them, and that Dennis could be absorbed into it without stress. She had been accepted into a local technical school to take a secretarial course but, more importantly, arrangements had been made with the psychiatric outpatient department of the local hospital for her to participate in group counselling for parents who had abused their children.

There were no funds available from any source for Dennis to receive private psychiatric counselling for the abuse *she* had received. Nonetheless the parole officer, an experienced woman and skilled counsellor, was confident that Dennis would gain insight into her behaviour in the group setting, not only regarding her own offence but also why she had chosen to put herself in such a disastrous situation at the age of sixteen. The board gave Dennis full parole, confident that she would never be back.

Steve Connolly at twenty-two had a long history of incarceration. He had had five juvenile detention-centre placements before he was fifteen, when he had graduated to provincial jail.

When the board saw him at Springhill medium-security institution in Nova Scotia, he had served one-third of a four-year sentence for drug-trafficking.

Connolly was the second oldest of five children. His father, a trucker, left home shortly after his birth but remained in the same coastal New Brunswick town. Connolly saw him around town a bit, knew where he lived, and occasionally spent an hour or so with him.

Connolly's mother was an alcoholic. A stream of "stepfathers" flowed through the house siring children as they went. These children were not beaten or sexually assaulted: they were simply neglected at every level.

From the time they were two the children had to more or less fend for themselves. Sometimes there was food and sometimes there wasn't. Sometimes the house had heat and sometimes it didn't. Sometimes there were clean diapers and sometimes there weren't. Sometimes their mother was there and sometimes she was gone day and night. When this happened she locked the children in the house with Connolly in charge. At one time the situation was reported to welfare authorities and the children were placed in foster care, except for Connolly, who was sent to stay with his paternal grandmother. After two months, during which time Mrs. Connolly dried out, found her Saviour and was born again, if temporarily, the children were returned home.

Connolly slid into crime as naturally as a seal into water. He started by stealing the small change from the pants of his mother's lovers, moved on to snatching purses, and graduated to joyriding in stolen cars.

Placed in the local juvenile detention centre, he was astonished to find a nice clean bed, a hot shower every second night, and three square meals a day. Returned to his community, he lay low for a while. Then one night he climbed through the roof of the Royal Canadian Legion hall and made off with some benefit funds. He wasn't surprised when the Mounties came around shortly afterwards and delivered him once again to the juvenile authorities. After another, slightly longer sojourn at the centre, Connolly returned home with the equivalent of a diploma in crime and a network of contacts with fellows like himself.

Having lived off his wits all his life, and lacking any moral and social training, Connolly found a natural outlet for his entrepreneurial skills and anti-social thinking in drug-trafficking. He was good at it. He started in a small way with marijuana but soon moved on to cocaine. By the time he was picked up he was a trusted member of an inter-provincial network.

He did not look threatening. He was thin and bony, with a sallow face topped by pale ginger hair. As he leaned forward, his hands tucked under his legs on the chair, you could feel him summing up the three board members, his narrow brown eyes darting back and forth like busy lizards.

With an inmate like Connolly it was impossible to develop an atmosphere of trust and confidence. His deprived childhood had forced him to develop values and behaviour that enabled him to survive, but which were criminal. Sitting opposite him with our leather briefcases, well-cut suits and subtle pieces of gold jewelry, we represented an alien world to him. We were part of the power parade that had passed him by since his infancy, stopping occasionally to intervene briefly in his life with our irrelevant views of the right way for him to act. We were part of the police, foster parents, children's agencies. We were part of "them".

It was hard not to feel we were wasting our time with Steve Connolly and with others like him. For him, crime was his life, his job, his "profession". He was aware of no social or moral conflict, nothing but a distant fear of getting caught. He saw the world in terms of black and white. "We" had money and goods and it was up to him to get his share. If he didn't help himself nobody else would. He was immune to psychological counselling. He believed everyone had an angle and he was skilled at manipulation. In his lifetime he would be in prison as much as he would be out. His various romantic liaisons would produce several children, for whom he would feel not a whit of responsibility.

The legacy of his parental deprivation dominated as we went through the board criteria, some of us aware of a tendency to take particular care to give him a fair hearing, as if we could now make some amends for society's indifference towards him as a child. His needs then must have been obvious to someone: in his erratic school attendance, poor grades, lack of medical and dental care, sleepiness during class, no lunch or lunch money, dirty clothing. Was every adult around Connolly blind to the evidence of his abandonment?

Now here we were fifteen years later asking, straight-faced, questions such as had he gained "the maximum benefit from incarceration?" — knowing that he was incapable of benefiting from incarceration unless someone took him apart psychologically and put him together again with some social values. Perhaps in his forties he would be capable of "benefiting from incarceration", having become fed up, burned out, and at last willing to try to find some legitimate means of support.

Would it help Connolly to be "reintegrated into society" if he were released at this time? No, it would not, for Connolly had never been integrated into what is normally meant by "society". And, finally, would Connolly's release constitute "a danger to society?" You could count on it.

Connolly had the wits, toughness, and type of character to survive and create a life for himself. Even though it was a criminal life, it gave him a sense of identity, of belonging to a group, of self-esteem. Why should he give that up and become a nothing in a society whose values were alien to him and whose behaviour he despised?

Decision: parole denied. Connolly's response: "That's awright. Didn't think youse guys would give me a break anyway."

Pierre Joseph Ryder scarcely fit into the category of abused children if we think of abuse as persistent, and sometimes deliberate, cruelty. But his story illustrates a common cause of great pain among children: maternal abandonment. When this pain is ignored and untreated, it can cause considerable psychological damage and social alienation even when the child has been adopted into a loving family. I saw a fair number of such cases in prison — inmates caught up in the search for the lost mother, the nurturer, the dream goddess, the one who would console, comfort, and accept.

Ryder was born to Marie-Andrée Gagnon, who lived on a farm outside a small village, one of hundreds in Quebec with the name of an obscure saint long forgotten in the rest of the Christian world. Gagnon was one of seven living children; to feed them, her parents worked like serfs.

Gagnon was smart, pretty, and ambitious for a better life. She chose "get away" subjects in school — typing, shorthand, and bookkeeping, and at sixteen she started work in Lac St. Jean. By seventeen she had moved to Quebec City and by nineteen she was in Montreal leading the life she had dreamed about — a room of her own, movies twice a week, sometimes a new dress, and money to send to her mother.

At twenty Gagnon married Paul Tremblay, a man ten years her senior. She was eager to have her own home and children. He was a poor choice: Tremblay was in the first stages of alcoholism, a fact that Gagnon chose to overlook.

By twenty-five she was the mother of a four-year-old daughter and a three-year-old son. Her marriage was a disaster. Coarse and abusive, Tremblay started to batter her. Too proud to return home, where there were no resources in any case, Gagnon endured as best she could, grateful only that her husband never abused the children. When she threatened to leave with them, Tremblay warned her that he would kill her if she did.

She believed him. One night she disappeared, leaving the

children behind. After that Tremblay's drinking increased. A few months later, unable to manage, he gave the children to the child welfare authorities for adoption.

The girl, Chantal, was pretty, charming, and highly adoptable. The boy, Pierre, although handsome, had turned into a bedwetter, runaway, and chronic whiner since his mother had deserted him. There were several offers to adopt Chantal but nobody wanted the boy. The adoption society remained firm: the "family" could not be broken up. Whoever took one child must take the other.

Finally the Ryders, a childless Ottawa couple who desperately wanted Chantal, agreed to adopt both. With considerable effort they set out to ensure that both felt equally loved. Chantal turned out to be all they had hoped for, but Pierre was another matter. At age five he got on a bus and was found later by police in Toronto. He said he was looking for his mother. By the time he was seven they had cured him of his bedwetting and much of his whining, but he was manipulative and secretive and he frequently ran away. His anxious parents punished him by spanking him, by depriving him of television; nothing did any good.

At fifteen Pierre started smoking marijuana; at sixteen, following a break-and-enter into a neighbour's home, he was on probation; by seventeen, despite his parents' vigorous opposition, he had left school and was taking whatever jobs he could find to pay for the drugs he was now hooked on. Soon after, he drifted away from Ottawa and disappeared. By then his adoptive parents, although anguished, were too worn out to really care.

We put the above facts together from information on file and the interview that followed our hearing with Ryder, who, at the time of our meeting in Cowansville prison in Quebec, had served one-third of a four-year sentence. His offences consisted of a series of break-and-enters in the Eastern Townships.

Ryder looked like a good possibility for an early release

program. His stealing was a direct result of his needing money for drugs, and he now seemed committed to going straight. Equally, if not more, important was that, while waiting for trial at Parthenais jail in Montreal, he had managed to contact his natural mother, who had remarried. Her name was now Collins, she lived in Winnipeg, and she had three more children, now teenagers.

This contact had had a profound effect on Ryder. He had formally expressed regret for his crimes in court — an act viewed with contempt by inmates — and had worked consistently since the start of his sentence to turn his life around. He had joined Narcotics Anonymous, and according to the NA's group director showed a good understanding of his personal and addiction problems. He had enrolled in academic upgrading and had passed grade twelve, was on a waiting-list for a woodworking course, and had become deeply involved in athletics to offset the debilitating effects of his former drug-taking. His attitude was unfailingly courteous to both staff and inmates, and he had no institutional charges in his file. He was for the first time taking responsibility for his own future.

His release plan was simply to go home to his natural mother and find employment wherever he could while going to night school. Mrs. Collins had written to say she would welcome him and there would always be room for him, perhaps in the house, but if not there in a small trailer in the backyard where he could have his own "little apartment".

"This next case looks quite positive," I said to Ryder's team before the inmate's appearance. "All reports are excellent."

They agreed, but Ryder's parole officer hesitantly offered bad news. "I just got a call last night from his mother. She doesn't want him. She has three teenage children, and apparently her husband never was that keen about having her child by her first marriage back living with them. She's worried about her 'own' children and by the fact that Pierre's been in prison, and that maybe this will get her other children going in the wrong direction. In other words, she doesn't want to risk anyone messing up her cozy set-up."

"I can understand that," I said reluctantly, "at least to some extent. How did Pierre take it?"

"He doesn't know," said the PO. "I only got the call last night and I haven't had time to see him since. But in any case, the mother swore me to confidentiality. She doesn't want Pierre to know she doesn't want him. She said she tried to tell him — they've not met but have spoken several times on the phone — but that she just couldn't do it."

For over a year and a half Ryder had obsessively devoted himself to becoming a son worthy of his long-lost mother, and now she didn't want him. This, I thought, was going to be one hell of a hearing.

"Let's see him, then," I said. I couldn't have imagined what was to follow.

Into the room bounded a tall, fit man of nineteen. His green prison outfit was clean and freshly pressed, a green baseball cap sat jauntily on his thick, fair curls. He came right up to our desk and triumphantly announced, "I've found my mother!"

We asked him to sit down and tell us about it, and to explain how he had used his time since coming to prison. He went through the list of his accomplishments, and volunteered the realization that it was despicable to break into people's homes and steal their goods. He had done it to get enough money to buy drugs but that, too, was in the past. He was now eligible for full parole and, having made maximum use of his imprisonment, could gain nothing further from being locked up. His voice was spontaneous, happy, and confident.

"I've read the pamphlets you send out," he said, "and I meet all your requirements for parole."

"Well, you've taken the right steps," I said, stalling for time. "But as to whether you're ready for parole, that's for the board to decide. Your plan is to go to your mother's?"

"Yes," he said. "I didn't apply for day parole so I could finish my grade twelve and I didn't want to go into a halfway house anyway — not now that I've found my mother."

"Unless there are exceptional reasons for doing otherwise, we usually first grant day parole, even though an inmate has reached full parole eligibility," I said. "If we did decide to grant you some form of release, there are a couple of good halfway houses in —"

"There's no need for me to go to a halfway house," he interrupted. "I've got my mother. Geez, I don't know why you're talking about halfway houses when I can go home."

"What about your other parents?" I asked. "Your adoptive parents? Have you been in touch with them?"

Ryder looked at me with quiet distaste. "Yeah," he said, "I wrote to Mum and Dad about a year ago and told them about finding my mother, and wanting to go to her. We've written a few times since and they came up here once to visit me. They were real happy, the way I've changed, and they said as long as I stay okay there's a place down there for me. But it's like I told you, I want to go to my real mother's in Winnipeg."

"Do you remember her?" I asked.

"Nope," he admitted, blushing. He stayed silent for a moment. Then he said, "My Mum and Dad, they've been good . . . but Chantal's why they took us. Nobody has to tell me that, I've always known it. That's one of the reasons I want to see my real mother, not knowing my father either . . . not knowing who I really am."

"Look, Pierre," I said, "you've done extremely well. And I hear what you say about wanting to be with your real mother. But maybe it wouldn't be the wisest thing to do." I could see the light going out from his face, the curve of his smile hardening to a thin line. I ploughed on. "She's had her own life now for many years. She has other children. Maybe it would be best not to go there right away but to wait a bit. With three children, and a husband, she has her hands full, and if she has a normal house one extra person . . . Well, maybe you'd be better off elsewhere."

He shoved his chair back and stood up, his voice raised. "My mother wants me and there's room. I can prove she wants me, it's in all her letters. Let me prove it. I'll go get her letters from my cell."

A few minutes later he was back, and one by one we read the letters in silence. It was all there, Ryder's mother's initial joy at hearing from him, the euphoric relief of being able to "explain" her abandonment of the children, the pleasure of his understanding and his manly assurance that forgiveness was not necessary. And then her slow reassessment, apprehension for what her prisoner-son could bring into the lives of her clean, law-abiding, high-achiever children, not to mention what unknown tensions his presence could cause within her marriage. And then the final determination — overlooked by the wishful Ryder — that she could not risk all she had for this unknown inmate who happened to be her son.

We turned the letters back to Ryder and watched as he carefully put them together and tied them with a ribbon. Then he said, a little aggressively, "You can see she wants me home, it's in every letter."

"Your mother's very fond of you," I admitted in response. I then asked him to leave the room while the board made a decision.

It took my board colleague and me, along with the PO and the LUDO, a good half-hour to hammer out a reasonable solution to Ryder's dilemma. We all were in agreement that he was at his optimum point for release. He had used all the facilities available to rehabilitate himself and a refusal now would be severely discouraging. We also agreed that Ryder's mother should have to accept some responsibility for her son, although we recognized that her concerns for her family were legitimate.

We decided that Ryder should get full parole. The PO agreed

to call the Winnipeg parole office and explain the circumstances of the case to them. If they were agreeable to taking it, it would be necessary to find accommodation in a suitable private home close to where Ryder's mother lived, perhaps in the home of a member of a community service club like Rotary or Kiwanas. It would also be necessary to interview his mother and have her attend at least a couple of sessions of professional counselling to arrive at a better understanding of Pierre's obsession and what she could do to help him. The same counsellor could work with Ryder toward an acceptance of his mother's situation. All this would be arranged through the Winnipeg parole office.

We could not vote for a parole until all these arrangements were agreed to by all parties. The only thing left now was to break the news to Ryder that his parole would be subject to these conditions.

When Ryder came back into the room, he flopped into the chair without taking his eyes off the board. After acknowledging the progress he had made, I went on to say that we didn't think he should go to live with his mother. He stood up immediately, about to protest, and refused to sit down.

Leaning across the desk, his control beginning to slip, he said, "I've done everything I'm supposed to do, everything. What's with you? You've read the letters. Are you trying to tell me she doesn't want me? Right from the start you've been against her." His voice was crackling with frustration and anger.

"If you sit down I'll finish what I'm trying to tell you," I urged. "Cool it, Pierre. There's a lot at stake, don't blow it now." He sat down.

I continued. "As I was saying, everything looks good — except your release plan. Going to your mother's home is not a suitable plan. You don't know one another. There's a lot between you still to be worked out. We are making arrangements for the Winnipeg office to find you a suitable place close to where your mother lives. If this can be worked out, and we see no reason why it can't be, we'll be voting for a full parole with two special conditions. First, that you abstain from all drug use, and second, that you participate in family counselling at the discretion of your parole supervisor.

"We're putting in the second condition because it is obvious from your mother's letters there is a great deal of affection between the two of you. But affection by itself doesn't solve everything. You need to get off on the right footing. With any luck it should take only a few days to make these arrangements; then we'll vote, and you'll be notified of the results immediately."

Ryder sat in silence, digesting the fact that he was at last getting out of prison. Minutes ticked by.

"Is that it?" he finally said.

"That's it," I said, "except for wishing you good luck."

He turned and walked out. As he passed through the door he paused, wavered, then over his shoulder came a begrudging "Thanks."

This was one of the few cases that I followed. A community-minded Winnipeg couple, with two teenagers of their own, provided Ryder with room and board in an area close to his mother's home. A few meetings with his mother put an end to his obsession. Although they got on well, his long-held fantasy of her lost its power. With time the two developed a genuinely supportive but casual relationship.

Obviously, not all abandoned children become criminals nor were all criminals abandoned as children. The fact remains that Canadian prisons are filled with a disproportionate number of adults who have suffered as children deep wounds at the hands of their parents. These wounds have festered with the years, have become infected with pain and rage, giving society another anti-social young offender to deal with.

I often think of childhood victims like Francis Roberts or Steve Connolly or Mary Elizabeth Dennis when self-styled "responsible citizens" urge the government to "get tough" with inmates. These responsible citizens would do more for society if they got tough with governments and with officials who fail to provide the funds necessary for adequate family support and child care.

8   *Skinners*

When I joined the parole board I thought of rape as vaginal penetration of the non-consenting victim by the offender's penis, which is the essence of the legal definition. I did not realize that this is often only a small part of what happens during a sexual assault — and that it may not be the most dehumanizing part.

The first few sexual assault cases in which I was involved included punching and kicking, anal penetration, throttling, repeated forced fellatio and cunnilingus, slapping and beating the head until the victim is semi-conscious. I soon realized that this spectrum of brutality is what rape is. When we read of a woman being raped in an underground garage, or of a man being sentenced to prison for rape, we are reading of a crime in which the victim might well have also been viciously beaten and forced to play out the offender's fantasies of pornographic violence.

According to a recent report released by CSC, there were 12,991 inmates in custody and 8,231 on conditional release as of March, 1989. This number included some 1,230 sex offenders in federal penitentiaries, and an additional 740 or so out on parole. This indicates that, in early 1989, approximately one out of every ten inmates in federal institutions was a sex offender.

Most sex offenders leave prison untreated. In early 1986, the year for which the most complete and latest figures are available from Correctional Service Canada, there was a total of approximately 345 rapists, and 255 other sex offenders such as incest cases, pedophiles, and molesters, in the federal system. The numbers receiving treatment at the time the report was written were seven rapists and three other sex offenders in the Kingston Treatment Centre; five rapists and seven other sex offenders in the Saskatoon Regional Psychiatric Centre; and eleven rapists and five other sex offenders in the Pacific Regional Psychiatric Centre in Matsqui, B.C. Even taking into account the fact that over a year there would be a higher number treated than indicated at any given moment, these figures reveal that at any one time the percentage of sex offenders receiving psychiatric treatment is negligible.

At any given time there are 250 incarcerated sex offenders in the Prairies region who would benefit from treatment at the Regional Psychiatric Centre at Saskatoon, a $50-million treatment facility completed in the early 1980s. Only 50 sex offenders a year, however, can be treated there, two groups of 25 inmates on a six-month program.

In the Kingston Regional Psychiatric Centre, one range of 16 cells for sex offenders has recently been expanded to 32 cells. However, the centre is short of nurses: this place is as mouldy and as miserable a dump as can be imagined. As of March, 1989, there were only 8 inmates enrolled full-time and 11 part-time in the sex-offender program. This program runs four to five months but individual programs of three to four months are sometimes arranged.

The total number of sex offenders in the Ontario region averages something like 230 in any given year. With a total of only 19 inmates receiving help, it is apparent that the majority of sex offenders in the Ontario and Atlantic regions, which this facility also serves, are going back into the community untreated.

At the Pacific Regional Psychiatric Centre, which runs a variety of programs, including one for very aggressive individuals, the sex-offender program is two years long, and can accommodate a total of 30 every second year.

It is surprising how many people believe that sex offenders sentenced to prison have to "undergo" treatment. It does not work like that. Inmates themselves decide whether or not they want to receive treatment, and they decide whether or not they want to stay in the program. Of the 30 patients now occupying beds at Pacific RPC, one-third will quit before the year is out, another third will stay between one and two years, and another third will stay beyond two years.

Formerly most sex offenders were sent to the same institution within their own region, but for the past two years the CSC administration has been trying to move away from specialized institutions to more homogeneous prisons. From a cost-effective viewpoint this might be a creative move, but from any other viewpoint it is a dangerous step backward.

A sex offender who mixes with the general population does not want his offence to be known, or he's fair game for a brutal beating. At the very best, he will lose whatever sense of security he's managed to maintain in prison. Prisoners at Bowden and at other prisons where sex offenders are among general population know which day the prison's health unit does the assessments for the Regional Psychiatric Centre, which offers special programs for sex offenders. Inmates avoid going to the health unit that day because they don't want to be pegged as sex offenders.

The bottom line is that most sex offenders are released back into society with the same psychological and attitudinal problems that caused them to commit their offences. This is not entirely the fault of Correctional Service Canada. Some experts believe that, despite problems, the CSC has some of the best psychiatric facilities and treatment programs in Canada. Nonetheless, while the programs offered are representative of the best known methods of treatment, there is still a wide diversity of views as to how effective they are. CSC has no follow-up support programs in the community nor are there, to my knowledge, any follow-up studies of former RPC patients to assess the long-term effectiveness of RPC programs.

Whether the programs are highly effective or only partially effective, the reality is that many sex offenders themselves refuse to become involved in treatment. Prison staff have little leverage, and no authority, to coerce them. The parole board's only leverage is to deny release to those who refuse to make any serious attempt to address their problems. When the board does this, it is simply postponing the real problem: the inevitable return of the untreated sex offender into the community.

Once they are released by the system, there is virtually no possibility that such offenders will obtain the type of long-term, intensive treatment available to them in prison; in any case, they are unlikely to seek it. They might become involved in an hour or so of psychiatric care weekly, but few ex-inmates can afford even this. The CSC, on special request by the parole board, can underwrite the costs in critical cases, but it is understandably reluctant to do so.

In any case, effective treatment must be voluntary. Yet the sex offender, in my experience, was the least likely of any type of offender to seek help, either before or during incarceration. Denial, defensiveness, habitual evasion of uncomfortable facts, shame and embarrassment: these all keep the sex offender from seeking treatment.

Derek Eaves, a psychiatrist formerly with the Regional Psychiatric Centre at Matsqui, B.C., believes there is another critical reason why these offenders avoid treatment. Now director of the Forensic Psychiatric Institute at Port Coquitlam, B.C., Eaves is of the opinion that placing a medical treatment centre in a maximum-security prison setting, as is the case of all three of Canada's forensic psychiatry centres, is counterproductive. Many offenders who need treatment are already living in medium- or minimum-security conditions. If they choose to go to an RPC, they are forced to relinquish the privileges that go with lower security, and to return to the restrictions of a maximum-security setting.

This is only part of the problem. Everyone who works in these psychiatric centres, whether doctor, nurse, or guard, is an employee of Correctional Service Canada, and the structure of the centres is strongly hierarchical; it is not the more egalitarian ambience desirable in a treatment setting. Trying to create a hospitable environment that instils a sense of mutual trust, and of working together towards rehabilitation, is virtually impossible when those who treat are also those who keep. In the RPC-penitentiary system, "confidential" patient reports are available to prison authorities and shared in detail with members of the parole board — who then can use the material against the inmate. As a result, a built-in barrier exists between inmate-patients and staff, who, as employees of the CSC rather than independent professionals, are often mistrusted by inmates as agents of the state.

Eaves believes that the solution to the problem of fitting a medical treatment centre into a prison setting is to divorce the psychiatric centres from Correctional Service and place them in the hands of national Health and Welfare authorities and staff — an unlikely scenario in view of CSC's track record for empire building.

There is little to distinguish the potential rapist from anyone else while he's on the outside. Once in the structured environment of a prison, however, the rapist often begins to exhibit characteristic personality traits. The show of remorse that he may have exhibited during his trial has often evaporated by the time he reaches parole eligibility. He has become defensive, sometimes going so far as to deny the offence took place, or to downplay it, shifting the responsibility for the crime onto others, especially the victim. "She asked for it," he'll sometimes tell the board with breathtaking ease, and when the facts are laid on the table he may dismiss them as "exaggerated".

He may aggressively deny that he needs any treatment,

claiming that he now has all the "insight" necessary to avoid raping again. Perhaps he will take a few months' treatment at the Regional Psychiatric Centre and then drop out of the course, claiming it was all "a waste of time". Or he will be "born again" as a Christian, and claim that it is now against his religion to discuss past "failings", which have now been "washed away by grace". If he has stuck with the sex offender program, he may roll buzz phrases like "insight", "self-understanding", "improved ability to communicate", and "assertive not aggressive" off his tongue like marbles off a board but be little affected by his treatment.

In my role as a board member, I formed the opinion that many sex offenders, and in particular rapists, will turn themselves inside out to avoid revealing or facing the truth about themselves. This perception supports the studies of experts who believe that those who interview sex offenders for assessment purposes will fail to make any worthwhile contact with the real person unless they adopt a tough, authority-based approach along with a degree of scepticism and cynicism. Although I thought this approach rather rigid and preferred to respond to the individual rather than to a stereotype, I had to admit there often *was* a stereotype, not in age or education, profession or appearance, but in the stunning self-centredness of the offender.

The four composite cases dealing with sex offenders I have created below will illustrate the different attitudes towards rape that are still commonplace among the public and the police, as well as highlight the fact that, for the victim, the offence itself is often only a part of the trauma.

Bruce Quinn was born in Windsor, Ontario, the youngest of two children. His father, who owned and ran a high-quality hardware store, died when Quinn was seven and his mother took over the business, leaving him in the hands of a series of housekeepers.

Lacking adequate guidance and support, Quinn began to chum around with a delinquent crowd and to adopt their values. To give him a fresh start, Mrs. Quinn sent her son to California to stay with his maternal grandparents when he was fourteen. The grandparents tried to bribe him into good behaviour with lavish gifts. Their indulgence only added to the problem and Quinn ended up quitting school halfway through grade ten. The grandparents sent him back to his mother, who by then had sold the business, remarried, and was living in Toronto.

After living with his mother and stepfather for a year, Quinn left home. He supported himself with low-paid labouring jobs and drank heavily. He was charged once with shoplifting, and a year later with stealing an automobile. He was fined on the first count, and acquitted on a technicality on the second.

At the age of twenty, Quinn married Susan Beckworth, a bright and ambitious woman three years older than he was, who managed to motivate him sufficiently to obtain a real estate licence. To his surprise, Quinn found that he liked selling real estate, and that he was good at it. Within four years he had built up an extensive clientele in commercial real estate. He was attractive, smart, socially smooth, ambitious, and far less concerned about ethics than about profit. He saw in real estate not only a chance to become rich fast, but also a chance to vindicate his past failures.

Quinn's fifteen-hour workdays and his drinking led to problems in his marriage. Eventually Beckworth walked out, and at twenty-six Quinn found himself alone again. This time, however, he was well-dressed, had a stylish apartment, and an air that said money was no problem. His heavy socializing and drinking increased, while his office performance declined.

One evening after several of the staff had been working late, he offered a co-worker a ride home. Jane Langdon was single, thirty-four, and well respected in the office for her competence and professionalism. While en route to her home, Quinn stopped at his own apartment, saying he was going on to dinner and wished to make a quick change of clothes. Langdon agreed to come in, and waited downstairs in the living-room while Quinn went upstairs to change.

A few minutes later he appeared on the stairs clad only in his briefs. Astonished and confused, Langdon grabbed her coat and made for the door. Quinn reached it before she did, and told her no harm would come to her if she took off her clothes. She refused, trying to push past him. He pushed her back towards the couch, beating her about the head and face with his fists.

Langdon once again refused to undress, and Quinn threw her to the floor and started to kick her. He then dragged her across the floor to the kitchen, took a knife from a drawer and held it to her throat. She agreed to undress on the condition that he put the knife away. Quinn then led her upstairs to the bedroom, forced her to commit fellatio, which he followed with penetration. He then allowed her to dress and drove her home.

Once in her own apartment, Langdon immediately called a girlfriend who lived downstairs, and she called the police. Langdon was taken to a local hospital, examined for evidence of rape, and later released. Quinn was arrested within the hour.

Quinn was granted bail — with the restriction that he did not make any contact whatsoever with the alleged victim. It took a year for the case to go to trial, and although Quinn denied his guilt on the stand, he was sentenced to five years.

Quinn applied for a temporary absence program after he had served two years of his sentence; he had been eligible for full parole four months earlier but prison staff had discouraged him from applying for it. He informed the board at the interview that he had filed an appeal against both the sentence and the conviction. He maintained that he was innocent, and that the victim had been a willing partner. He claimed that no threats had been made and that no knife had been used. He pointed to the fact that he had driven the victim home as proof of the consent of both to the incident. We informed him that the question of his guilt or innocence had been a matter for the court to decide, and that we fully accepted the court's decision: it was not our role to do otherwise.

Quinn came across as an assertive and cool young man who sought to control the interview. He quietly interrupted any reference to the offence by saying, "The Appeal Court will decide about that." Although he was articulate and appeared to be psychologically open — shaking our hands, making eye contact, volunteering the frank admission that he had been living in the fast lane — he adamantly refused to accept any responsibility for the offence.

He had as his assistant James Kedwick, a former colleague in the realty business. Kedwick had recently formed his own company and he was willing to employ Quinn on his release. Like Quinn, Kedwick appeared affable and, in some undefinable way, slick.

Quinn offered his own version of the offence to the board. He said that Langdon had shown a strong sexual attraction toward him long before the incident occurred. He said that she had made a point of hanging around his office, coming and going constantly, and even bringing him coffee when it was not her role to do so. Questioning revealed that certain office records were kept in Quinn's room and that it was necessary for Langdon to "come and go" in the normal course of her own job. Furthermore, it turned out that the office coffee pot was plugged in immediately outside Quinn's office, and that it was quite normal for workers to poke their heads around the corner, ask Quinn if he wanted coffee, and bring a cup in.

It wasn't only the way she came and went, said Quinn, it was the clothes she wore, and the way she walked out of the office, "sort of sashaying". Furthermore, she was single, and it was "obvious" to Quinn that she was on the lookout for "a little action".

Quinn said that on the evening of the "alleged" offence, Langdon spent considerable time working on files in his office and he felt sure she was seeking his attention. When he suggested driving her home, she immediately agreed even though Quinn said he had to stop at his home first. "If she hadn't really wanted to go to my place," said Quinn, "she could have given me the message then. But she didn't."

Quinn said Langdon was lying when she told the police that she was shocked when he appeared before her undressed. He claimed that they had agreed she would get undressed and that when he came downstairs she'd be "ready". "I said — with a sort of grin — 'I'm going upstairs to change.' And she smiled back and said, 'O.K. And I'll be waiting for you down here.' It was totally clear what she meant. But when I got downstairs she was still dressed, and I was the one who was surprised. I told her that and she said something like, 'Well, I'll come upstairs with you then.'" When asked whether he thought that Langdon had been teasing him, he said carefully, "That thought did strike me."

When asked about the report on him prepared by the prison psychiatrist, Quinn started chewing his lower lip. "Well," he said reflectively, "he said actually I was pretty normal. I explained to him that I'd taken a phony rap for this woman." He lapsed into silence. After some prodding Quinn reluctantly continued. "I've never had any trouble with women. I've always been able to get a woman if I wanted one."

Probed about the breakup of his marriage, Quinn said that he didn't blame his wife for leaving him and admitted that his drinking had occasionally led him to beat his wife.

The psychiatric report showed that Quinn's father had been a heavy drinker. In fact, complications from alcoholism had contributed to his early death. When drunk he would beat his son on the slightest provocation. Afraid of her husband, Mrs. Quinn had not intervened until the beatings had progressed to a dangerous level, and her son hated and despised her for not protecting him. When his father died, Quinn felt an enormous relief, followed by guilt at his reaction. He turned to his mother for confirmation of his self-worth, but this was not forthcoming. Instead, concerned about her family's future, Mrs. Quinn left her son to the care of housekeepers, all strangers, and devoted herself to saving the family business. She had probably loved her son but she was under severe emotional stress and ignored his needs. As a result, he had a highly conflicting attitude towards women. He was fearful of their power over him: he found competent or authoritarian women particularly threatening. Over the years he adopted an aggressively "macho" stance to help control his sense of inner fragility and insecurity.

The psychiatrist said he believed that Quinn was guilty of the rape, despite his denials, and advised treatment so that Quinn could avoid committing similar acts of violence against women in the future.

I asked Quinn again how he felt about the psychiatric report. He leaned forward and looked earnestly into my eyes. "The psychiatrist is entitled to his opinion," he said. "It doesn't mean he's right, though. It doesn't mean that I raped anyone."

"Mr. Quinn, you've been in prison for two years and you have done nothing to gain any self-understanding. You obviously have an unresolved alcohol problem — you've stated yourself that your drinking was getting out of hand — and now you want to go back into the community on a series of passes. What have you done to earn them? What assurance does the board have that you won't do the same thing again?"

"Well, I won't," he said flatly.

"So you did do it."

"I didn't rape her," he shot back. "She'd been asking for it."

"She told the court she wasn't the slightest bit interested in you, that she simply accepted a ride home, and genuinely believed you had to stop at your place to change before going on. She said she struggled to get away, and only submitted when you held a knife against her throat. You did have a knife, didn't you?"

There was a moment's silence. "Yes," he said. "But I was just fooling around. She was teasing me, pretending she didn't want it, and I was teasing her."

There was no hope of Quinn's seeking help, or of his benefiting from psychiatric or psychological counselling, until he faced the reality of what had happened that night. Had it happened before? Was Jane Langdon only one of several women who had been similarly attacked by Quinn?

On the other hand, Quinn had been on bail for one full year before his trial and sentencing. During that time he managed to bring his drinking under control and was not involved in any new incident of sexual assault. If he could retain control for a year, perhaps he could do so for a lifetime.

In the end, the board rejected his application for a temporary-absence program. In another case for a lesser type of offence prolonged good behaviour might have led to a positive vote. But Quinn's offence was serious, and he refused to acknowledge his guilt. Furthermore, the court had been aware of his bail performance when it sentenced him to five years' imprisonment, so we could not place too much value on it.

Quinn did not seem surprised to be denied. He asked when he could see the board again, and what was it the board expected of him. We told him it would be useless to apply for any release program before he had served another year, as he would need at least that much time to undergo a treatment program. "We want you to understand clearly that before the board will consider any release you must seek help for your alcohol addiction, and you must consider going into the sex-offenders program at RPC."

"I'll never do that," he said at once. "*Never*. There's counselling available here. If I need it, I could get some help here and work the rest out for myself. I'm not a nut and I won't go in with a lot of other nuts."

I did not see Bruce Quinn again, but over a year later a fellow board member told me that he had sat at Quinn's next hearing.

Quinn, whose appeal against sentence and conviction had both been rejected by the Ontario Supreme Court, now admitted that he had used force and had threatened Langdon with a knife. He admitted to assaulting women in similar circumstances before. He was as good as his word, however, when he had told us that he would never go to the RPC. He was determined to stay in prison until his mandatory supervision date rather than submit to having someone "play head games" with him.

François Bertrand was thirty-six years old when he applied for day parole after serving just over three and a half years of a seven-year sentence: three years for indecent assault, and four years consecutive for buggery. He had originally been given a five-year sentence but this had been raised to seven years on a Crown appeal.

The police report on the sexual assault read as follows:

At 16.30 hrs., May 10, 1983, Mary Watkins of 3452 Wylin Avenue attended at the above office and stated that her son, James Fox Watkins (04 May 1977), had been assaulted by an unknown individual of uncertain age. Cpl. Weaver attended and Cst. Meakins took a statement from Mary Watkins. She said an unknown individual had approached the victim Watkins at approx. 15.40 hrs. as he walked past Connaught Park to his home two blocks away at 3452 Wylin Avenue after playing with friends under supervision of the City Recreation Department. Said unknown individual enticed the child Watkins to his car by stating that his mother was waiting there. The child followed, and in the car said unknown individual forced Watkins' head down and attempted to place his penis in the child's mouth. Watkins cried, and the man told the boy he didn't have to do it, and thereupon released the child who ran home and informed Mary Watkins, who immediately attended at above station. A limited description of the assailant was taken by Cpl. Weaver, and Mary Watkins and the victim were driven home by Cst. Meakins. A police check of the entire area was immediately made without results.

The police report on the buggery charge stated:

At 19.20 hrs., July 9, 1983, François Bertrand was driving on Highway 2 approximately 40 kilometres north of Calgary when he picked up a male hitchhiker, George Donald (08 Jan. 1969). Donald asked to be dropped off in the Bowden area and, on arriving at said location, attempted to leave the auto. At this point Bertrand automatically locked the door and sped off at high speed. Donald did not struggle as he was confused as to Bertrand's intent.

According to victim Donald, Bertrand drove north for approx. three minutes then turned off the main road and drove down a deserted farm track. Here he ordered Donald out of the car and told him to remove his pants. When Donald refused, Bertrand attempted to do so himself. In the ensuing struggle Donald managed to escape and fled across a field but was outrun and caught by Bertrand, who threw the boy onto the ground, twisted him onto his stomach, and committed the act of buggery. After this Bertrand dragged Donald back to the car and attempted to force Donald to assume the dominant role. Donald was "in a daze" (possibly severe shock) and could not do so. Bertrand then demanded that Donald commit fellatio on him. Donald was in severe pain and said he could not do so.

Bertrand then allowed Donald to dress, drove him back to the Bowden area, and released him. Bertrand warned Donald not to tell anybody what had happened to him or he "would pay for it". Donald walked to the home of his aunt, Mrs. Daisy Pateau, 89 Forsyth St., with whom Donald lives. On being told of the events Mrs. Pateau notified police.

Donald was able to give a statement to the two attending officers, Cpl. Hoschuck and Cons. Wolkins, with a detailed description of the assailant and his auto. Donald was then taken by Cpl. Hoschuk to the Calgary General Hospital and was there examined by Dr. M.P. Oswell, who confirmed that Donald had been raped. Donald was admitted to hospital at 19.30 hours and surgical procedures to correct the severe tearing of the anal tissue were scheduled for the following day.

News of this rape spread throughout the small community with the result that the victim Donald has suffered much public humiliation to the point where he has dropped out of school and refuses to leave his home. Donald is also subject to nightmares and the family is attempting to arrange for some help from the Calgary Mental Health Association.

Bertrand was apprehended in a bar at 860 Davies St. at 23.10 hrs., July 1, 1983, obviously in a state of extreme intoxication. He was taken by Constables Bretnick and Miles to this office, where a statement admitting to the offence was made by Bertrand at 23.53 hrs. On further questioning Bertrand also admitted to the May 10, 1983, assault of James Fox Watkins.

The parole board files and the psychiatrist's report showed that Bertrand was the youngest of five children. His father had died when he was four and he and an older brother were given to an uncle and aunt to be raised. They could not deal with the child and placed him in a Catholic orphanage at the age of six. He remained there until the age of twelve when he ran away. Although he had made sporadic contact with his mother and older brother, he had been essentially on his own on the street since twelve, earning his living in a series of low-paid casual jobs and as a prostitute. From the age of sixteen, he became more involved in prostitution, but at the time of his arrest had not been actively engaged in it for some time, being fully employed for the last five years as a window dresser for a downtown department store.

Bertrand had told the psychiatrist that he could not remember ever being happy, that even as a small child he had felt angry. He recalled having been sexually molested by one of the Brothers at the Catholic orphanage. He did not report the incident at the time because he was too confused and embarrassed.

The psychiatrist reported that "Interestingly, when Bertrand was approached for the second time by the same person he said he was not interested, but he gave the name of another boy whom he claimed would be. This was a lie to escape the Brother's further attention, and Bertrand admitted to experiencing 'great guilt' over having done this to the other boy."

In the years that Bertrand was in the orphanage his mother visited him only twice. After he ran away he was befriended by a Catholic priest in Toronto, with whom he had a brief sexual relationship which was followed by a non-sexual friendship. Bertrand drifted back to Montreal where he worked as a prostitute, and finally moved to Calgary where he "hoped to change his life". This reformation apparently took time, as Bertrand spent some months in Headingly Jail after being sentenced for possession of stolen goods. He stated that in jail he lived in fear, was beaten, and finally reluctantly resorted to giving sexual favours as a means of protecting himself.

Bertrand recounted that he had had his first heterosexual experience when he was fourteen. In Calgary he attempted to change his homosexual pattern by dating two women, both of whom he said "were quiet types but fun to be with".

Bertrand had been working full-time for about a year and was occasionally dating another woman who became pregnant by him. The woman had an abortion, which Bertrand said led to his becoming impotent with women and gradually returning to his former homosexual behaviour. Bertrand's sexual ambivalence resulted in a marked deterioration in his capacity to cope with any form of stress. He started drinking heavily and after the incident with the Watkins child — which he said was a single incident committed impulsively when he saw the child alone on the street — he considered suicide.

On the day of the assault on George Donald, Bertrand had been unexpectedly fired from his job. He was given no explanation other than that his work was no longer satisfactory. Loss of employment and the abrupt severing of contacts with fellow workers was experienced by Bertrand as "losing the only normal life I'd ever had". He felt extreme humiliation, anxiety, and believed he no longer had any control over his life. He went to a local bar, started drinking, and stated on arrest that he had virtually no memory of the attack on Donald.

The psychiatric report, completed just two weeks before the board's scheduled parole hearing, concluded:

> Mr. Bertrand was interviewed prior to his going to the Regional Psychiatric Centre and following his return after one year of treatment. At the time he was admitted to the RPC Bertrand was assessed as having numerous conflicts about his sexuality. He was dominated by a fear of rejection, his judgement was impaired, he had no appreciation of the consequences of his actions, and he had little understanding of the disinhibiting effects of alcohol on his personality.
>
> Mr. Bertrand was seen after his return from treatment and seems to have developed considerable insight into the causes of his violent sexual behaviour. He became a serious member of Alcoholics Anonymous in RPC and I believe he has come to understand the destructive role that alcohol, his own fears of rejection, and his need for security and affection have played in his life.

He also appears to have discovered that, although his childhood was marred by various unhappy and disturbing events, he nevertheless gained certain decent values and standards. Some of these have been in violent conflict with his homosexual tendencies, others will probably serve him well and give some direction to his life provided he abstains from alcohol. With few opportunities to relate to women, he has reverted to homosexual behaviour, and although he still has some conflicts regarding this he seems to have a much more accepting and realistic attitude towards it. He still maintains some fantasies about having a heterosexual marriage with a wife and family and a little house, but on the other hand he recognizes that he is more attracted to men than women.

I understand that while in RPC he developed a friendship with a man of his own age. This man, doing a sentence for embezzlement, had been previously married with a family, but the marriage had failed due to his homosexual tendencies. Bertrand and he have acknowledged a mutual sexual attraction and are considering setting up house together when both are free to do so. This friendship has helped Bertrand to overcome his deep sense of inadequacy and to see himself as an acceptable person.

It is my opinion that the Watkins incident was not part of any pedophilic pattern but resulted from the combination of unresolved sexual problems, heavy drinking, exceptional stress, and impulsiveness. Bertrand's only prior offence was for possession of stolen goods. He has no criminal record of deviant sexual behaviour and it would be unusual for such a pattern to develop at the age of thirty-two. The assault on Donald was also committed when Bertrand was in a state of intoxication and under extreme stress. It is worthwhile noting that police did not lay any other charges against Bertrand, or accuse him of any unsolved prior incidents of assaults on children, if such incidents existed. Bertrand has told me that both acts were isolated events, and I tend to believe him.

In my view Bertrand has made considerable gains and, with the proper structures, is likely to continue to do so. Despite the brutality of the assault on Donald, Bertrand does not have the marks of an aggressive personality. He has many attributes that will assist him in his eventual return to the community, including a desire and the capacity to be self-supporting. The central question is Bertrand's use of alcohol but he appears to be a committed member of Alcoholics Anonymous. The prognosis in the short term is excellent and I believe the possibility of recidivism at long term is unlikely.

A psychology report from the RPC sex-offender program included a summary of Bertrand's history, his pre-treatment assessment, treatment, and post-treatment assessment. The pre-treatment psychometric assessment showed that Bertrand had some problems with assertiveness but on the Buss-Durkee Hostility Inventory showed high scores on resentment and guilt. The Thorne Sex Inventory also presented high scores of sexual maladjustment, frustration, and impulsiveness. On the Personal Reaction Questionnaire, Bertrand showed high anxiety, instability of moods, and tension. On the Sexual Knowledge Test he scored 60 percent. The Wechsler Adult Intelligence Scale (revised) yielded scores in the high average range (110).

In the pre-treatment physiological assessment Bertrand's arousal profile indicated that he did prefer males to females, although adult females of his own age evoked some sexual response.

Bertrand's treatment to date had been aimed at bolstering his low self-image and increasing his sexual knowledge, increasing his ability to respond to hostility in an appropriately assertive manner, reducing the use of defense mechanisms to avoid anxiety, decreasing impulsiveness, and building the habit of examining alternatives when making decisions.

The post-treatment psychometric assessment showed considerable change. There was an increase in assertiveness and a marked lowering of passive, frustrated/aggressive response. Guilt and anxiety had both been reduced, primarily because of the marked gains made in sexual adjustment.

The post-treatment physiological assessment indicated no response to a series of slides of five-, eight-, or twelve-year-old males and females, minimal arousal for females of his own age, and the strongest response to a thirty-year-old male. There was no inappropriate response to either male or female teenagers.

Bertrand had passed his parole eligibility date sixteen months earlier. He had served forty-four months and would be released on mandatory supervision when he had served fifty-six months of his eighty-four month sentence. He had been out of prison with a group under escort for swimming and fishing excursions in remote areas about an hour from the prison. Having now completed the sex-offender program, Bertrand was applying for day parole to a halfway house in Calgary. Calgary police had been contacted to see if they had any objection to his returning to the community where his offences had occurred. They had replied that as long as a special condition to refrain from alcohol was placed on Bertrand's parole certificate, they had no objection.

After a lengthy interview with Bertrand, the board was in favour of a program that would support Bertrand's efforts to rehabilitate himself, but not necessarily day parole. Bertrand was not defensive; he accepted full responsibility for his offences and expressed profound remorse for his victims. He outlined the steps he had taken in prison to prevent a recurrence. Besides the year spent in the sex-offender program (which he himself had sought after incarceration), he had upgraded his basic reading and writing skills, which were formerly at grade four level; developed an interest in woodwork, for which he showed considerable talent; and now hoped to obtain a job in a related field on the outside.

The three board members believed that a release on day parole was unsuitable; Bertrand still had twelve months to go to his MS date and any release earlier should be slow, structured, and closely supervised. We recommended an unescorted temporary absence (UTA) program, starting with perhaps twenty-four or thirty-six hours once a month for six months. Day parole could then go into effect after Bertrand had proven he could cope outside without alcohol.

Unfortunately, the halfway house that Bertrand had chosen was one of several across Canada that refused on policy to take sex offenders. Bertrand had no family, and no one willing to take him overnight once a month. His only outside contact was the director of the prison AA program; all of his former work colleagues and friends had deserted Bertrand following the publication of his offences.

In addition to our decision to deny day parole, we also voted to delay, for a maximum of three months, the UTA program, until suitable accommodation could be arranged. We hoped that a suitable AA sponsor could be found to participate in Bertrand's gradual release.

One month later Bertrand was released for twenty-four hours to the home of Herb and Mary Stanton. A community assessment showed them to be a stable, common-sensical, childless couple, both fifty-five, with sufficient room to accommodate Bertrand overnight. Neither had any police record. They were considered good neighbours and good employees. Herb Stanton had had a drinking problem but he had been a member of AA for twenty years. Simple in their tastes and direct in their speech, the Stantons were endowed with a marvellous capacity to accept other human beings and, in accepting, often to heal. With the best of the parole service and prison staff members, people like the Stantons are the unsung heroes of the criminal justice system.

Christopher Windsor was the archetypal rapist: the quiet, unseen predator who sights a desirable victim, tracks her to her home, makes sure she is alone, and attacks her.

When I met him, Windsor had already served seven years of a twelve-year sentence. He was now thirty-two, fit, tanned, and strikingly good-looking. There was not the slightest hint in his fine-featured face, firm mouth, and easy smile of his deeply sick mind.

He was picked up by police in a small prairies motel in the mid 1970s following the rape of a sixty-two-year-old woman driver who had given him a ride as he hitchhiked. When he was apprehended, he did not deny having had relations with the victim. On questioning he admitted to "showing" her a hunting knife, but denied that he had threatened her, stating that the mere fact that she had picked him up indicated she was "willing". He saw no incongruity in a sixty-two-year-old woman supposedly desiring a twenty-five-year-old stranger.

When asked whether he had raped before, Windsor stated he had never raped anyone. He said he had had sex with "three or four women drivers" who had stopped to pick him up, but by doing this they'd shown "interest" and were therefore "willing". The police report of Windsor's statement noted that Windsor "was co-operative, easy on himself in that he lied all the time, and seemed to feel nothing for his victims."

A police check showed that Windsor had started his career as a rapist at eighteen, when he had picked up a hitchhiker, raped and sodomized her. He was inexplicably acquitted of the charge. His second rape charge came one year later, when he followed a nurse who had been working a late hospital shift down a quiet residential street late at night and assaulted her in a deserted lot. Again, he was acquitted.

Police records indicated no charges of rape, or any other

offence, were laid against Windsor for the next eight years, when he was picked up in the prairie rapes. Further inquiries, however, revealed that Windsor had spent one of the intervening years travelling around Europe, as well as one in the United States and one in Britain. In Britain he had accumulated two assault charges, both against women, both of which appeared to have been rape attempts. He had been sentenced to a term of three months and deported back to Canada.

When apprehended for the prairie rapes Windsor at first denied committing any other rapes. After receiving his twelve-year sentence and being told that the sentence would not be increased, Windsor wrote out a long statement for police in which he admitted lying when he'd denied previous rapes, and confessed to "at least a dozen other rapes". He had raped in several major Canadian cities, using a variety of techniques to gain access to women's homes. He had raped one sleeping woman after creeping through a ground-level window, another by scaling the drainpipe and forcing the second-floor sliding-glass doors, another by pretending to be a jogger and accompanying the victim back to her home, and another on a date.

Windsor's usual approach was to force himself upon the victim in a straightforward sexual act. If she resisted, he did not punch or kick her, but coolly showed the knife he always carried and told her coldly and calmly that he was ready to use it. "But in fact," Windsor's report concluded, "I never harmed any of them." Pressed, he added, "Unless they lied to me." When this happened he "punished" them by forcing them to participate in extremely degrading sexual acts.

What were the causes of Windsor's need to rape and terrify women? After studying the entire case, including five psychiatric reports by three different psychiatrists at different periods, two excellent psychological reports, and innumerable institutional and other reports, the roots of his disturbance were still unclear.

The reports agreed that Windsor was a hyperactive, energetic individual. He was impulsive, with a low tolerance for frustration. Although he had been raised in an apparently "normal" family, with an older sister and a younger brother, he had always caused trouble both at home and at school. At seventeen, against his parents' wishes, he had left school; at nineteen he entered a marriage that lasted eighteen months. He had been charged with his first rape during this period.

The reports also agreed that Windsor was emotionally shallow. "We started talking about violence towards women," one psychiatric report stated, "and he became emotionally blocked immediately. His face became distorted and he had difficulty controlling his tears. He looked like the picture of remorse until he said: 'I can't stand being rejected.' He immediately started talking about his mother and the fact that it was she who had decided that he should be sent to boarding school. 'It was like putting a knife in me,' he said."

Another psychiatric report stated: "Windsor has an average intelligence, his memory is intact for recent and remote events, and he seems to have some insight into his behaviour. He appears unwilling or incapable, however, of working through the meanings of these insights. His moods on the whole are very labile: one moment he was near tears about his offences, but when I switched the subject he lapsed immediately into a smiling and joking response."

The psychiatrists reported that Windsor viewed women as inferior creatures best related to by aggressive acts. When the victims submitted to his aggression, Windsor would excuse the assault, claiming that the women were "whores" who had initiated sex with him. The words they used to describe Windsor included "egocentric", "amoral", "compulsive", and "without guilt".

The psychiatrists arrived at the same conclusion: that Windsor was not a psychotic or even neurotic individual; he merely suffered from a "personality disorder". (I thought him dangerous and crazy.) He was also impulsive, aggressive, unfeeling, and asocial, and "no amount of punishment or imprisonment would likely make any difference to his behaviour."

Although Windsor had entered the sex-offender program at the Regional Psychiatric Centre of his own volition, he lasted only five months before fleeing back to regular prison on the pretext that RPC was making him worse.

In the board interview, Windsor put forward a strong case for some relief from imprisonment. According to institutional reports he had no charges, he had made "some" effort to understand his behaviour and to change it, he had worked at improving communication with staff and other inmates, and he needed a pass program to "keep his family intact".

Yes, Christopher Windsor had a family. Two years after he started his twelve-year sentence, the prison warden had given Windsor permission to marry a twenty-four-year-old legal secretary whom he had met before his last arrest. The warden had granted Windsor two escorted temporary absences to his wife's home in the previous year, when the couple had conceived a child.

Now Windsor was asking the parole board for a limited program of unescorted temporary absences to his home "to help maintain family involvement" and to "help prepare for release on MS". Windsor had only one year to go before release.

Staff were unanimous in supporting the UTA program. Dangerous though this man was they had a point: if Windsor was simply dumped on the street after eight years of incarceration his chances of succeeding would be slim. If he could be "eased back in" in short, supervised, controlled doses the chances of his stable, well-planned re-entry would be increased.

Yet, if we granted Windsor this program and he raped again, it was unlikely that the media would have the time, or interest, to search for the reasons why the parole board had voted to release such a dangerous individual. The board's action would be condemned out of hand. By keeping Windsor in until his MS date the board would avoid being held accountable if Windsor reoffended.

Our final decision was to grant a UTA program of forty-eight hours a month to go into effect six months before Windsor's MS date. Windsor's destination was his wife's home, where, for the first three months, he was to remain all weekend. If this program went satisfactorily, it was to be expanded to forty-eight hours a week, and normal outside activities, such as shopping, would be permitted. A special condition was imposed forbidding the use of alcohol or drugs.

Because Windsor was so dangerous, police in his area were specifically notified of his impending release as well as the conditions of that release. Two weeks after Windsor's MS went into effect he was charged with sexually assaulting a teenage woman who happened to smile at him as she crossed a supermarket lot. Although the charge was thrown out of court because the victim was too frightened to testify, the board revoked Windsor's mandatory supervision and he was reincarcerated. He has since been re-released back into the community.

Gino Dampierre was a thief by occupation. "It was my job, my profession," he told police after he was finally caught. He slept during the day, the curtains pulled in the bachelor suite he rented in downtown Regina. At about 5 p.m. he got up, showered, dressed, and ate a light snack. (He didn't like eating heavily before he went "to work". It was easier going up and down drainpipes and into basement windows on an empty stomach.) And as he crept around inside homes and apartments — sometimes pausing to gaze upon the sleeping residents — he liked the feeling of being light, sleek, and cat-like. When he finished what he called his "night shift" and returned home, he'd eat his main meal of the day, do his household chores, watch a video movie, and go to bed. A prison psychological report described him as "an extremely well-adjusted individual".

On the night of March 23, 1983, the twenty-three-year-old Dampierre got up at 5 p.m. as usual, showered, and prepared for work. There was nothing in the police report to indicate what tools Dampierre took with him, but it was noted that when he attacked his victim he was wearing a black ski mask and gloves.

He drove his old van to within walking distance of an apartment building that he had cased the previous week, a three-storey building with a lot of single residents. The building was being cleaned by sand-blasting, and scaffolding criss-crossed the front of it, which gave easy access to the apartment balconies and their sliding-glass doors. It was Friday and there would be enough money from cashed paycheques to make the job worthwhile.

Dampierre was not a classy criminal by inmate standards, merely a common thief who was quite satisfied with cash, some jewellery, and a few saleable odds and ends like transistor radios and watches. He had done so many B&Es he couldn't count them and yet he barely had an adult record. Years earlier in Ontario he had done nine months at the correctional institution in Guelph, on four B&E charges, and later in Vancouver he had served six months at Oakalla.

The night of his last arrest Dampierre had already "done" three apartments, while the owners slept unawares, and he was in a fourth when the absent owner returned. He heard the key in the lock, and had time to hide behind a door in a small utilities room before a woman of about thirty-five entered the bedroom, carelessly kicking off her shoes, throwing her coat onto a chair and her clothes onto the bed. Taking her time, she dressed in a nightgown and went to the bathroom. Returning a few moments later, she got into bed and switched off the light.

Dampierre waited silently for the woman to fall asleep. From his hiding-place, he could see her form stretched out under the covers, and his thoughts began to stir. He remembered the images in a porn magazine that he had flipped through earlier that evening. As he waited alone in the darkness, the power of the images grew.

"I didn't mean to hurt her," he later told police. "I'd been reading this magazine and it got me thinking. I thought she might want it herself. But she woke up and saw me and started to scream. I guess my balaclava frightened her. I put my hand on her throat just to stop her yelling. I didn't want to hurt her. I panicked, I guess that's when I squeezed her neck. If she'd kept quiet and just did what I wanted she'd have been all right. She coughed like she couldn't breathe, so I sat her up and patted her on the back. I put on the light, and made sure she was all right, and then she lay back real quiet and I did it."

After raping his victim, Dampierre pulled her phone from the wall, warned her not to call the police, and fled in his utility van. He was picked up by a cruising police car five blocks from his home.

Dampierre was a classic example of the B&E thief who turns, without premeditation, into a rapist. Because of the bruising on the victim's throat, he was charged with attempted murder, rape, and burglary. When the case went to trial he was portrayed by Crown counsel as a highly assaultive sex offender, despite the lack of a sex-offence record. The result was an aggregate sentence of twelve years.

His reputation of being a violent rapist preceded Dampierre to prison. For the first two years of his sentence, he had lived in imminent danger from genuinely violent inmates who wanted to match their reputations against his. Finally, he requested and was given a cell in the protective custody range. Once out of protective custody, Dampierre had been set upon by other inmates and raped.

The board considered Dampierre's previous criminal history, the offence itself, the amount of violence he had demonstrated in the offence, and the fact that, while the robbery had been planned, the rape had been opportunistic. We questioned Dampierre to see how much responsibility he accepted for the offence, and whether he had used either drugs or alcohol before committing it. We noted that there was no evidence of any preoccupation with deviant sexual behaviour, and that his exemplary institutional behaviour under extreme pressure indicated an ability to develop and maintain stable social and work relationships. He had upgraded himself academically and passed his grade twelve, had completed a small motors repair course, and had become the chairman of the prison Alcoholics Anonymous group. Although Dampierre did not have an alcohol problem, the AA philosophy helped him gain self-knowledge.

While none of these activities guaranteed that Dampierre would become a pillar of society, they indicated his strong motivation to change. Our interview with him reinforced the impression that prison had provided Dampierre with an opportunity for growth and he had accepted it. Occasionally this did happen, particularly with young men who were able to receive both counselling and trades training. Dampierre had been taught a bitter and harsh lesson and had proved himself tough and flexible enough to benefit from it.

Dampierre was given day parole to a halfway house. Six months later, when I was working in the same region, his file was passed on to me for a "paper" vote regarding his application for full parole. By then he had done well for over four and a half years of his twelve-year sentence. During his day parole his behaviour had been excellent. He was still involved in AA, and had found employment in a store that sold automobile parts, where he enjoyed the work.

Ex-inmates often experience a bitterly hard time finding work. If they are honest about their records with their potential employer, they are often rejected. But if they hide their records, they live in fear that one day they will be exposed. There are a few malicious police officers whose hobby it is to make life on the street tough for parolees. They follow ex-inmates from one place of employment to another, tipping off the boss or harassing the ex-inmate just enough to ensure that he will be let go.

One such officer had gone to the trouble of dropping by the store to inform Dampierre's boss of his record. The gesture backfired. Dampierre had already informed the employer that he had a a record. Accompanying Dampierre's application for full parole was a letter of support from his boss.

Three years after Dampierre was given his full parole, I was waiting for the lights to change in the middle of Saskatoon's shopping district when I noticed a young couple standing beside me. They were happily fussing over a newborn in a stroller. The man was clutching a huge bag of Pampers in one hand, while the other rested over his wife's on the stroller. I knew I'd seen his face before and later that afternoon the name came back — Gino Dampierre.

There is a litany of phrases that rapists use to explain why they attacked their victims. High on the list is the notion that if a woman is out alone at night she is secretly inviting a sexual assault. Whenever I go into an underground garage, or walk down a deserted street at night, or find that I am suddenly alone in a shrub-lined park, I remember this, and wonder who is out, untreated, now.

9 *Fraud: The Middle-Class Crime*

There are a great many ways to practise deception for unlawful gain. Much of this fraud is hard to detect, costly to uncover, difficult to bring to court successfully, and impossible to prevent. Police say that the cases that end up in court are only a fraction of the fastest growing crime in the country.

The fraud artist, the swindler, the con man all share certain skills. They are usually well mannered, relatively intelligent, amusing, likeable men and women. They are skilled at developing relationships of trust, even affection with their victims, whose subsequent feelings of betrayal poison and often destroy their lives. Fraud is not, as some have called it, a "victimless crime". Among elderly victims, who are the prime target for many scams, stress-related illness and premature death are not exceptional.

The general term "fraud" is commonly used to denote the simpler forms of what are called "economic crimes". These can include the failure of large investment trusts resulting from misuse of investors' funds and misrepresentation of the accounts of the trust, or activities that result in the laying of charges such as "fraudulent manipulation of stock exchange transactions", or "using mails to defraud". Hundreds of investors, many with limited life savings, may be irreparably damaged by their losses. Such people are every bit as traumatized as they would be by a break-and-enter followed by a savage beating. At least if they had been robbed and assaulted they would be regarded as victims rather than as fools.

The amount of talent and effort required to commit many such crimes is often greater than would be required to operate an honest business, or to work as an ordinary employee. Some fraud schemes require highly sophisticated technological knowledge; others are as simple as writing a bad cheque. Yet for repeat-offender swindlers, fraud seems invested with glamour and excitement; it's a common observation among prison workers, who see the same old faces coming in and going out, that the fraud artist is as addicted to cheating as the alcoholic is to the bottle.

If a person wants to get something for nothing, he or she can cheat on an expense account or manipulate the stock market. Most people who work have a chance to steal or defraud, however junior their jobs. Serious business fraud, however, is usually committed by executives and managers simply because they have more opportunities than other subordinates to rip off their employers or the system. When they do steal or embezzle or defraud, the breach of trust is that much greater.

Can the criteria the parole board applies to most inmates be usefully applied to convicted fraud artists, dishonest trustees, and others who have committed some breach of trust? Can the board sensibly ask whether the applicant for parole has "learned his or her lesson", and whether granting parole would put society at risk? Should other criteria apply to such cases, and if so, what should they be?

These questions arise because the criminal justice system makes a distinction between violent and non-violent crime, and generally treats non-violent crime more leniently. After I had been on the parole board a while, I ceased to be surprised at meeting men who had been convicted of a major fraud spending much of their time playing golf or tennis in minimum-security institutions, and confidently coming up for day parole or a generous unescorted temporary absence program with the full support of their team after serving one-sixth of their sentence.

Just as there is a legitimate question as to whether the criteria for release used by the board in dealing with violent offenders are relevant to the release of fraud artists, so is there a question as to what should be expected of the fraud artist once he is imprisoned. What sort of a rehabilitation program should he be expected to undergo; what retraining, what psychological self-understanding should he be expected to gain while he's locked up and playing golf at public expense, while his wife on the outside is often struggling from day to day to survive?

Fraud artists like to be liked: within the prison community they will organize the social events. They will initiate projects to work with the aged, or with retarded children. They will run the Christmas missions. They will be in Toastmasters, or involved with the Jaycees. They will deal with prison staff in an equal-to-equal manner: watching them, it is impossible to tell who is the staff member, who is the inmate. They are popular with most staff and guards because they conform to the rules and never cause trouble. They will even have some staff members happily do little extra things for them, and are sincerely hurt and bewildered when other staff members accuse them of manipulation.

Hidden under their cheerful, loquacious fronts, however, are grudges, the same sort of chip-on-the-shoulder attitudes so commonly found among young anti-social inmates. This attitude could best be described as a belief that they deserve more out of life than they have, that life somehow owes them, and that it was all right to take what they want from those who have it. They appear to feel no guilt whatsoever about this; on the contrary they seem to believe they're correcting an unfair balance. They have little ability to grasp how others suffer at their hands. Although their talents may be misspent, these men and women are not lost, confused, deeply wounded people who can be guided by firm counselling and some insight into law-abiding lives.

It is difficult to give representative composite cases of the fraud artists I encountered. Many of the crimes involved such complex accounting manipulations that a recital of the illegal acts, and how they were detected and proven, would be tedious indeed. Nevertheless, I will attempt a few examples of cases that involved relatively simple deceptions.

Betty Carter worked for the Collins Transport Company, which operated a trucking terminal in Sherbrooke, Quebec. An accounts receivable clerk, she had been with the company for eight years and was considered an outstanding employee of unquestionable fidelity and trust. She rarely booked time off, and she frequently took work home with her to keep up to date.

Carter's main daily duty was to balance the cash with the pro-bills (sales invoices) and prepare a cash deposit for the bank in Sherbrooke and a cash report for processing in the Montreal head-office computer. She processed all incoming cheques from charge-account customers, by matching cheques to the applicable pro-bill control copies and preparing a deposit for the bank in Sherbrooke and a receivable report for Montreal. She then presented the deposit slips and receivable reports to the manager for his signature, along with the customers' cheques and cash in an envelope.

The supporting pro-bills were always in sealed and stapled envelopes. The envelopes were not opened and verified by the manager. If the total of the bank deposit agreed with the total of the receivable report, he would sign the report. One copy of the report, the bank deposit slips, and the pro-bills were then forwarded to head office, while a second copy of the report and the remittance copies of pro-bills were retained on file at the terminal.

Carter also worked on the accounts receivable aged analysis, a listing prepared in Montreal of all outstanding pro-bills. Frequently she would question certain delinquent accounts. She would often take the analysis home saying she'd been too busy to do it during the day.

In November, 1985, Carter became ill. After she was away a month, Collins Transport replaced her with Cecilia Black. With a colleague, Black began the collection work on the two largest charge-account customers, Happy Farms Produce and Mountain Stream Lager Ltd. Successful collection on these accounts would immediately reduce the sixty- and ninety-day totals on the receivable analysis, which had become very high.

Happy Farms Produce was advised that their pro-bills dated September and October were still outstanding on the receivables analysis, to which they replied that they had paid these invoices by cheques issued in September and October. Collins Transport then examined copies of the reports around the dates of the Happy Farms Produce cheques, together with cheque stubs and supporting pro-bills. Although the pro-bills that were paid with the Happy Farms cheques belonged to Happy Farms, they were dated June and July. Collins Transport wondered if Happy Farms had made an error, because their October cheque, which was paying September and October pro-bills, did not appear to apply to the pro-bills in the deposit, which were dated July and August. Happy Farms responded that there was no error on their part and that they could not understand how there could be a mistake because they had attached all the applicable pro-bills to their remittance.

Collins Transport then called Mountain Stream Lager Ltd. and asked for payment for their August, September, and October pro-bills. Mountain Stream said that only the current pro-bills for December were outstanding, and that prior pro-bills had been paid by cheques already issued and returned as cashed. When Collins Transport checked their copies of the reports, they found that the Mountain Stream cheques were deposited, but that the cheques were applied to older Mountain Stream pro-bills and other customer pro-bills and not to the pro-bills submitted with their cheque by Mountain Stream.

The pro-bills outstanding totalled about $39,000 at Happy Farms and about $16,200 at Mountain Stream Lager. At this point Collins Transport could not understand how these outstanding pro-bills could be cleared up. Head office auditors visited the Sherbrooke terminal and Happy Farms on December 18 and 19, 1985, and took all terminal reports and records back to their head office. It became obvious that the customer's cheques had not been applied to the pro-bills as intended by the customer. Instead they were applied either to the customer's older pro-bills or to *other* customers' pro-bills. Further investigation revealed that these other customers were cash-paying customers.

Collins contacted each customer, prepared a detailed list of each customer's prior pro-bills, plus a list of those pro-bills which Collins' books indicated were unpaid. When all the replies were in, it was clear that several pro-bills shown as outstanding had, in fact, been paid. It was also determined that the dollar value of the pro-bills that had been paid by these customers before December, 1985 (although still recorded as outstanding) totalled $110,349.20.

Collins Transport had fallen victim to a common fraud scheme known as lapping. Cash and cheques were received at the Sherbrooke terminal of Collins Transport and controlled by Carter. Carter had taken the cash, while the cheques were applied to the pro-bills which were to have been paid by cash. Consequently, the pro-bills remitted with the cheques remained outstanding on the accounts-receivable analysis published at the end of each month. Carter owed Collins Transport the full $110,349.20.

Carter was found guilty of fraud, and sentenced to two years, which she served at the Prison for Women in Kingston, Ontario. She had no previous convictions. A single woman, she had cared for her mother, who had died six years earlier. She had been a bookkeeper all of her working life. Until she stole from her employer, a process that extended over five years, she had led a law-abiding life. She had neither an alcohol nor a drug problem. She had invested some of the stolen funds in a town-house, but this property had to be sold at a substantial loss while she was unemployed and awaiting trial. After lawyers' fees had been paid, she had a total of approximately $20,000 left, which she had voluntarily paid back to the company.

Middle-class in her manners and speech, Carter had had an extremely hard time from some of the other inmates in Kingston, which houses the toughest women inmates in the country. She had lost thirty pounds through fear, tension, and ill-health. She had taken no courses and received no counselling while in prison. She had no explanation for her fraud other than the fact that promised pay raises had not come through, that she had felt underpaid, and had "given way to greed". When she started to work at Collins, she had had no intention to defraud, she said.

Her release plan was to go to an older sister's home in Sud-bury, Ontario (a community assessment on her sister was excel-lent), and to look for a job in that area. The only work she was trained to do was bookkeeping. She had lost her home and savings and at fifty she was worried about the future and her ability to look after herself. She stated that she would never steal again as she had "learned a bitter lesson".

The board granted Carter full parole. Although she had undergone no programs, the board felt she fully appreciated the gravity of her offence. Her sufferings in prison, and the fact that she would not be employable as a bookkeeper on release made it extremely unlikely that she would offend again.

Joseph Rozum was a professional con man who had lived on his wits all his life. He had been in and out of provincial jails but, until he was forty-two, he had never served federal time. His racket was simple and generally successful. His target was older women whom he bilked out of their life savings. Many of his victims could not face the ordeal of testifying. They were deeply ashamed of their own naiveté, and so strongly did they dread being publicly seen as incompetent in managing their own affairs that they often hid the loss from their own families and bore their pain in silence.

Rozum's technique was to go through the telephone book making phone calls to elderly women. Skilled and experienced, with a rich voice and creamy manner, he readily elicited from his victim the information he required. He gave his target a false name and said he was an inspector from "bank headquarters". To this line the woman often volunteered the name of her bank. Rozum would then say that the bank had discovered an internal theft problem. "We consider you a long-time and trusted customer, and we would like you to help us clear up this matter," Rozum would suggest.

He instructed each of his victims to go to her bank, draw out $2,000, and then go to a designated place, usually a shopping mall, where she was to hand over the money to a "bank employee" who would look after it. An accomplice would play the bank employee role, and tell the victim she would be notified and her money returned as soon as the bank found the culprit. It usually took over a week before the now anxious victim would contact the bank and learn that she had been swindled. When Rozum was apprehended, it was discovered that of eight known victims in one city, one had died, two were incapacitated with stress-related illnesses, three refused to testify because of their "shame" ("I feel I've been raped," one woman said), and two came forward, stating they wanted to see the so-and-so in prison.

Rozum received three years. He spent his time in prison happily organizing various events, and was liked by all for his cheerfulness and optimism. There he met a woman, Eva Alexander, who had accompanied a friend who was visiting an inmate.

Alexander, who appeared at Rozum's parole hearing as his assistant, was widely respected and liked in the adjoining small community. A widow in her early fifties, she was comfortably off and owned her own home. She was aware in broad terms of Rozum's current offence, and nobody, including the parole board, had either the right or the mandate to clarify the extent of his strictly confidential criminal history. She informed the board that they were to be married on his release.

Rozum did not give the board any reason to believe that he had changed his attitudes as a result of incarceration. He accepted little responsibility for his life-long fraudulent activities, and showed no understanding of the grief he had caused his victims. The board considered Rozum a high risk to reoffend and denied his parole.

Norman Conrad was a lawyer in Smiths Falls, Ontario. He had no previous record. His path had been straight and clear — from high school to Dalhousie Law School, to articling with a Toronto firm, to his calling to the bar. He was a member of several civic organizations and a respected figure in Smiths Falls, where he had taken over the practice of a retiring lawyer.

Conrad did well, but he lived beyond his means and felt himself to be under a vague but constant pressure. In his mid-forties, married with a family, he started "borrowing" by dipping into his clients' trust funds. At the same time he changed from being a light social drinker into a heavy user of alcohol.

Initially he made money on his lootings in stock transactions, but eventually the bottom dropped out of some utilities investments. An audit turned up the irregularity in Conrad's books and he was charged, found guilty, and received a stiff sentence of six years for defrauding five clients of a sum of approximately $150,000.

The judge had excoriated Conrad for his "betrayal of trust", for his "selfish dishonouring" of the legal profession, and for his "careless indifference" to his clients' financial fates. He pointed out that Conrad had no previous record, that he had suffered intense public humiliation, and had been disbarred for life by his profession. "Nevertheless," the judge stated, "the blow that you have dealt to the integrity and good name of your profession calls for a substantial period of imprisonment as a deterrent to others who might be tempted to follow suit. I would, however, have no objection to a release on parole when that is deemed to be appropriate." In essence, the court in its wisdom had decided to leave any decision regarding parole to the discretion of the board.

Board members had on file a document indicating that the provincial law society had levied a sum on its own members so that Conrad's victims could be recompensed for their losses. Also on file were letters from three victims telling of the months-long trauma they had endured, the ill health they had suffered, and their continuing sense of shock at Conrad's betrayal. They asked the board not to parole Conrad, stating that to do so would make a "mockery" of the law, and would encourage others in a position of trust to be tempted to commit similar crimes.

Conrad, now fifty-one, applied for full parole after one-third of his sentence. His prison behaviour was exemplary. He had completed a correspondence accounting course and had done well. He had no institutional charges, and had benefited so greatly from the Alcoholics Anonymous course that the outside volunteer who ran it had made him chairman of the group. There was no further program he could take, having participated in all the programs available in that institution.

Conrad's wife, who had been forced to sell the family home, decided after initial difficulties to remain in the marriage. She visited her husband three times a week. His three teenage sons visited every Sunday. His release plans were to return to Smiths Falls, where his wife now had an apartment and his brother-in-law, a successful manufacturer of quality leather goods, had offered him a permanent position running the small back office.

At his parole hearing Conrad spoke enthusiastically about his lifelong commitment to the goals of Alcoholics Anonymous. He expressed extreme remorse for his offence and a determination to rebuild his life. Both he and his wife, who accompanied him, said that they had learned to communicate more openly with each other since his incarceration.

Board members reached a decision in Conrad's case only after lengthy discussion. One member maintained that Conrad satisfied the three criteria for release, and that the victims' letters asking that Conrad's application be denied were secondary considerations. This member said that if the board gave Conrad day parole to a halfway house he would simply occupy a bed needed by someone else who had no family resources. As Conrad had a job waiting and could support himself and his family, there was no point in keeping him in prison at the cost of $40,000 a year, as he was not a danger to anyone. Full parole should be granted, he argued.

The second board member said that the criteria for release were ultimately only guidelines, and that when board members voted, their discretionary powers allowed them to consider the good of the community as well as the good of the inmate. Conrad had enjoyed a position of trust in the community, and he had caused much suffering and had degraded his profession by betraying that trust. This board member noted that the sentencing judge had specified that a substantial sentence was required as a deterrent to others: to release Conrad immediately at his parole eligibility would "bring the law into disrepute".

The board members finally reached a compromise decision, and voted to grant Conrad full parole that would become effective in three months' time.

The task of reaching a fair parole decision in cases of fraud is often complicated by the fact that application of the board's three criteria for release often unwittingly works to maintain the concept of fraud as a victimless crime. The introduction of a fourth criterion that would recognize the social damage done to corporations and communities, as well as the psychological damage done to individuals, in breach of trust and fraud cases would be useful in decision-making.

10   *Murderers on Parole*

The television cameras form a pushing, shoving circle around the victim's sister as she emerges from the Toronto court house. She looks dignified and satisfied. "The man who took my brother's life has been sentenced to life," she says. "Now that his killer has been permanently put away, I can start to put it all behind me."

Although the thought of someone being "permanently put away" may or may not be comforting to a victim's family, the fact is that no such sentence exists in Canadian law.

A life sentence can include the possibility of parole anywhere from seven to twenty-five years, depending on what kind of life sentence is given. This sentencing flexibility becomes clear as we look at some of the facts that surround the main offence for which a life sentence can be given: murder.

There are two degrees of murder, first degree and second degree. A conviction for first-degree murder is given in cases of planned or deliberate murder, contract killings, the killing of a police officer, warden, guard or prison employee. A murder is first degree if it occurs during a hijacking, a kidnapping, a hostage-taking, or sexual assault on a male or female.

All other murders are second-degree murders, although the charge may be reduced to manslaughter if the offence was committed under "sudden provocation" and "in the heat of passion", as specified in the Criminal Code.

Anyone convicted of first-degree murder receives a "life

minimum" sentence with a parole review at twenty-five years. (None of the 380 people who are presently serving this sentence are included in the examples that follow.) After fifteen years the offender can apply for a full judicial review of his case, so that he might be granted *eligibility* for parole. If this review grants eligibility, a hearing will then be scheduled by the parole board.

For those found guilty of second-degree murder, the sentence is also a "life minimum" term, with the judge setting the parole review at ten to twenty-five years. Statistics show that in 75 percent of second-degree "life minimum" sentences, judges set the parole eligibility date at ten years, while in 25 percent of the cases they set it somewhere between twelve and twenty years.

There is also a "life maximum" sentence. Under this sentence the inmate becomes eligible for parole after serving seven years. This sentence is not imposed for murder, but is often used in manslaughter cases — as well as in drug-trafficking, armed robbery, sexual assault, and occasionally break-and-enter cases.

When I first joined the parole board and saw one person getting three years for stabbing someone to death and another person getting six, or eight, or life maximum, or life minimum, I assumed that differences in circumstances, or some subtle points of law, of which I knew nothing, were involved. It turned out that in some cases there were, and in other cases there weren't. With some chagrin I realized just how much could depend not on law or on justice, but on the competence of one's lawyer, the energy of the Crown prosecutor, the availability of Crown staff to assist, the size of the court backlog, the disposition of the judge, and the willingness of both parties to plea bargain. Plea bargaining is a process by which the defense counsel and the Crown together work out an arrangement under which the Crown reduces the gravity of the charge laid and the sentence sought, in return for the defendant pleading guilty. This means that the case does not go to trial.

Take this hypothesis. A man sets out to kill his wife. He subtly presents her to his friends as "nervous, getting worse". He goes to the local police and confides that he is worried about his own safety. It's all fiction, but the police, not knowing either the husband or wife, record his complaint. Two months later the man kills his wife in "self-defence". He is charged with first-degree murder because all the evidence supports such a charge.

A year goes by while the accused awaits trial. Among the victim's friends, the subject has been worn threadbare. They want to forget it and get on with their own lives. Slowly, people adjust to the idea that the husband killed in self-defence, although at first the mere notion was seen as patently ridiculous.

Still, the police regard the killing as murder, first-degree, planned and premeditated for months. They have done an intensive investigation and hold out for the murder charge. But the courts are backlogged with cases for more than a year ahead. The Crown prosecutor is overworked. His staff is on holidays, ill with the flu, or tied up with other cases. The defence lawyer knows it will be in his client's interest to plead guilty to a lesser charge. His earnings in the long run will be as much if he spends one day in court with a guilty plea to a lesser charge, instead of three weeks on a trial that will involve considerable case preparation and will put the rest of his caseload into deep freeze.

The Crown prosecutor thinks of the two other homicides that have been waiting to go to trial for months, of the pile-up of break-and-enters, rapes, and assaults, of the enormous demands on his staff that the preparation for a first-degree murder trial will involve. So he and the defence lawyer sit down and hammer out an agreement in which the charge is reduced from first-degree murder to manslaughter in return for a guilty plea. The defendant gets a "life maximum" sentence and is eligible for parole in seven years, and the police are left wondering what their job is all about.

All those sentenced to life have one thing in common: they will never reach a mandatory supervision date or a warrant expiry date. They are under a life sentence until they die. After a fixed minimum period of imprisonment, they continue to serve their sentence in the community. They remain permanently subject to the control of the National Parole Board and the parole service. After an initial period of intensive supervision on the street, they will gradually earn increased freedom. (Intensive supervision means that the parolee is interviewed personally every fifteen days by his parole officer.) After a number of years, supervision may mean an interview once or twice a year. Parolees cannot change jobs, marry, or make any major move without the parole board's permission. If they become involved in any illegal activity, or if they start drinking heavily and alcohol was related to their original offence, or if their behaviour destabilizes, they can be immediately returned to prison without any charges being laid.

Our society has had great difficulty in coming to terms with a suitable deterrent, or punishment, for the taking of a life. The pendulum has swung in several directions over the years. For example, those sentenced to life for murder before January 4, 1968, became eligible for parole after seven years, but those sentenced to life for murder between January 4, 1968, and January 1, 1974, had to wait ten years for parole eligibility. Even a death sentence commuted to life, before January 1, 1974, allowed for parole after ten years. The present twenty-five-year mandatory sentence for first-degree murder, introduced in 1976 as a political trade-off for the abolition of capital punishment, is extraordinarily punitive by earlier standards. While first-degree murderers should be kept out of society, there is no consensus as to how long they should be kept out. The government has never proffered any theory or principle as to why it settled on twenty-five years as a mandatory term, rather than ten, fifteen, or thirty-five years. The question arises that if an inmate is dangerous after twenty-two years of incarceration, what will happen to make him safe after twenty-five years? If he is safe after ten years, why keep him incarcerated — unable to support his family and costing the state a minimum of $40,000 a year — for another fifteen years?

In the following case studies, which include situations in which there was extreme physical violence but neither murder nor manslaughter occurred, a marked disparity in sentencing for similar acts emerges. This disparity forms the background against which parole board members must make critical decisions regarding the release of inmates who have received "life" sentences.

Raymond Bouchard, nineteen, had no previous record. He was one of five children from a respected family in a small mill town. Three weeks before the offence he began dating a thirty-year-old woman of whom his parents disapproved, and he moved out of their home into his own apartment. This move was the culmination of bitter arguments that had gone on for two years between him and his parents regarding his frequent use of marijuana and hashish.

Bouchard and a male friend, both unemployed, got into an argument with two young men who had parked their truck in such a way that it blocked Bouchard's car when it was parked outside a local store. The two young men, aged eighteen and seventeen, apologized, and tried to take off. Bouchard remained argumentative, and one of the young men told him to "fuck off". They then got into their truck and drove away.

Bouchard chased them in his car, and produced a .303-calibre rifle, firing at them until the clip was empty. He then drew a .207-calibre rifle from behind his seat, and for the next ten miles he fired at the other youths' truck. Both men were wounded and will be partially handicapped for the rest of their lives.

Bouchard was convicted of attempted murder and sentenced to three years. When he appeared before the board for full parole twelve months after sentencing, he had no institutional charges, had completed his grade twelve, had excellent work reports, and he had benefited from regular participation in Narcotics

Anonymous. The shock of imprisonment had greatly matured him. He had sought but had been unable to get psychological counselling. His release plan was simply to return to his parents' home and seek employment.

Although Bouchard appeared to meet the three criteria for release, the board denied him parole on the basis that his release plan was unsuitable. The sentence of three years had been strongly criticized in the local press, and feelings about the offence ran high in the small community. Both victims were still receiving medical treatment and they and their families were the objects of sympathy and support. The board has no mandate to take the lightness or severity of a sentence into its considerations, yet in this case it concluded that to return Bouchard to a hostile community after one year would not assist his reintegration to society and might in fact set him up for failure.

The board felt that Bouchard should be encouraged in his efforts and would benefit from some relief from imprisonment, and suggested a limited unescorted temporary absence program to a halfway house in another community. Bouchard preferred to stay where he was and do his time. He was released to his hometown eight months later, four months before his mandatory supervision date.

Damian Cleaver, fifty-two, had been involved in an armed robbery thirty years earlier. He had served four years and was released by ministerial decision (this was before the parole board existed). Apart from two assaults and three drunk-driving charges — for all of which he received fines — he had committed no crimes.

After his release Cleaver spent a couple of decades in the merchant marine, and later worked as a bar waiter. In March, 1979, Cleaver and his girlfriend, Angela Riposo, threw a big party for all their friends. Cleaver and Riposo had lived together for eight years and had finally decided to marry. After their friends left, the couple continued to drink. What happened next is not known; Cleaver has no memory of the actual event. All he remembers is calling the police, who on their arrival found Riposo dead on the kitchen floor, apparently strangled. She was covered with a blanket and there was a pillow under her head. "She's all right, isn't she?" Cleaver asked. "I've tried to keep her nice and warm." Cleaver was convicted of manslaughter and sentenced to four years.

Cleaver was seen after serving sixteen months. Lifelong heavy drinking, and the loss of his fiancée at his own hands, had turned him into a lonely, regretful man, aged beyond his years. Although he was at his full parole eligibility date, he requested day parole to Osborne Centre, a halfway house in downtown Calgary. Apart from regular attendance at Alcoholics Anonymous, he had spent his time at Drumheller working in the kitchen, watching TV, and reading. He had no visitors and wrote no letters.

The board took into account several facts. One was that from the time of the armed robbery thirty years ago to the murder Cleaver had not exhibited any aggressive tendencies. Secondly, he seemed sincere in his involvement with AA. Thirdly, despite the availability of brew on the inside, there was no suspicion that Cleaver had been involved in manufacturing or distributing it, or in any other institutional breach of good conduct. Fourthly, he was genuinely remorseful about his offence. However, the offence showed that he was capable of extreme violence when drunk, and the earlier charges of drunk driving indicated that he had had an alcohol problem for many years.

The board concluded that Cleaver was not an undue risk to the community and that his determination to maintain sobriety could be tested best in the community while living under the supervision of the staff of a halfway house rather than by a later full parole or a release on mandatory supervision. The board granted Cleaver's request for day parole, and placed on it three special conditions: to refrain from all intoxicants; to stay away from all premises where alcohol was served; to continue his involvement in AA in the community for as long as instructed by his supervisor.

Dale Higgins, twenty-one, had no previous charges on his record, despite a harsh and turbulent childhood. His parents' marriage broke up when he was six and he spent the next four years in a provincial boys' institution, followed by two years in a variety of foster homes, and final placement in a group home. He worked occasionally, pushed soft drugs, and was using LSD at the time of the offence.

He was found lying in a snowbank by the police. Their reports described him as hallucinating, irrational, and confused. The officers returned him to his apartment as they feared he would die from exposure if he were left outside in the freezing cold. In the apartment on the living-room floor, they found the still-warm body of an eighteen-year-old woman. Examination revealed she had been stabbed once in the left side of her chest and had died from internal bleeding. Higgins said he had known the victim for three years and although he did not like her, he stated that he had no reason to kill her. He said he had just felt like killing someone.

Higgins was charged with murder on June 6, 1978. He entered a plea of not guilty, and his case was remanded from week to week. Five months later, Higgins appeared in the Court of Queen's Bench, the charge of murder was withdrawn, and he pleaded guilty to the lesser charge of manslaughter, for which he was immediately sentenced to eight years.

The board denied Higgins's application for parole. Although we had a full psychiatric report completed at the time of his admission to prison thirty-two months earlier, as well as the results of two psychological assessments done within the past year, no clear picture of the reason for his offence emerged. The psychiatrist held that the offence was the direct result of a bad LSD trip, whereas the psychological tests indicated deep feelings of anger and aggression, particularly towards women. The board believed that Higgins's statement — that he had "just felt like killing someone" — raised serious questions that required further consideration. His institutional performance, which included involvement in Narcotics Anonymous, had been excellent, but the board considered this positive factor to be far outweighed by the gravity of the crime and the questions that still surrounded it. In denying parole, the board ordered that Higgins be assessed by a complete psychiatric panel (two psychiatrists and one or two psychologists), and set a new hearing date one year ahead.

Richard Lachance, forty, had no previous convictions. He was a law-abiding man who worked long hours at his job as a plumber. Raised in poverty, he placed economic security above all other needs. He was a tense, driven person, with a limited ability to express himself or to communicate his feelings.

At the age of twenty-eight, Lachance married a woman of twenty. He encouraged her to continue her job in a local factory, with the result that the couple saw one another only at the end of a long day, and often not until late at night. After two years of this loneliness, Madame Lachance started going out in the evenings, at first with girlfriends, then with one or two men. One evening she came home, burst into tears, told her husband that she did not love him anymore and that it would be best for both of them if she left for good. She then told him to sleep on the sofa and closed the bedroom door.

For two hours Lachance sat on the sofa brooding and drinking. Then he went to a closet, took out a gun, went into his wife's room as she slept, and killed her with four shots. He was charged with murder, and sentenced to life minimum, with the judge setting parole eligibility at ten years.

The board met Lachance at the end of his tenth year at a minimum-security institution, Ste.-Anne-des-Plaines. Lachance started his sentence at Laval, but was soon transferred to Cowansville, a lower-security prison. There he had a total breakdown, and spent the next two years at Pinel Institute, a forensic psychiatric hospital outside Montreal.

After a lengthy interview, the board agreed with the conclusion of the psychiatric reports that Lachance had gained great personal insight into the roots of his offence — overdependency on women with extreme anxiety precipitated by the threatened loss of his wife — and that the long incarceration had both stabilized and matured him. Everything indicated that the likelihood of any further violence was negligible. These gains had been made in the first five years: for the last five, Lachance had worked in the kitchen, watched TV, and waited.

The board judged that there was nothing to be gained by prolonging his incarceration, but because Lachance had been locked up for ten years, a slow, structured release was essential. The program granted was in two stages: three months of escorted temporary absences for ten hours a week for social reintegration, followed by three months of unescorted temporary absences of forty-eight hours a month for employment search. If all reports were satisfactory, the board would then consider day parole.

Paul Andrews, forty, had a minor record but one that had been active for twelve years — two charges of theft, three years later a conviction on two charges of break-and-enter, four years later a stolen-auto conviction, and finally possession of stolen property. He obviously lived on the fringe of the law, yet had spent a total of only nine months in jail and paid out some $400 in fines.

On the night of the latest offence, he and an accomplice broke into the home of a forty-four-year-old man named Gerry Gibson. They beat him severely, tied him up with an electric cord, and loaded his record collection, stereo, television set, and video camera into their car.

Andrews then returned to the house and stabbed Gibson six times in the chest and shoulders with a six-inch-blade kitchen knife. Gibson was found two hours later by his sister. Rushed to the local hospital, he was transferred by helicopter to Toronto General Hospital, where his life was saved by a highly skilled surgeon, who remarked that Gibson was the fourth stabbing victim he'd saved that week.

Andrews was sentenced to six years for robbery — and one year concurrent for causing bodily harm with intent. Incarcerated in May, 1982, he became eligible for full parole in May, 1984.

The court had seen fit to give Andrews one year concurrent for the stabbing. Without the technical advances in cardiosurgery and the surgeon's skill, Andrews would have been charged with murder or manslaughter. However, weighing Andrews's luck was not part of our criteria, difficult though it was to ignore. Andrews had sought no counselling, seemed comfortable in prison, had little to do with staff, and a lot to do with the professional thieves. He told the board that he had no explanation for his vicious attack on Gibson, other than the fact that Gibson had verbally abused him. He said that he had not been armed, that he had taken the knife from Gibson's kitchen when Gibson continued to call him names. Andrews made much of this and seemed to think that his savage reaction to Gibson's name-calling was understandable.

The board denied Andrews parole. His self-excusing attitude towards the offence, his unwillingness to address his problems, and the intermittent activity on his record indicated that his values were criminally based. His exaggerated response to Gibson's verbal provocation indicated a low threshold of frustration, a dangerous capacity for violence, and unpredictability.

The board set a review for one year, and instructed Andrews to use any programs available to gain some understanding of his own behaviour. A year later Andrews had not fulfilled any of the board's expectations. He was again denied parole and was released on mandatory supervision in May, 1986.

Udel Kutaana, a forty-seven-year-old Inuit man, was a familiar client of the RCMP lockup in his Labrador town. He was a heavy drinker who tended to commit assaults when drunk, although when sober he was a model worker, husband, and family man. Kutaana's wife, Mary, was also a heavy drinker. On several occasions the local RCMP officer had rescued her from being severely beaten by her husband.

One day the couple and a family friend named Rudi Kemjaru had been drinking together. Kutaana went to tend to his fishing nets and when he returned home he found his wife having sex with Kemjaru. Kemjaru dressed hastily and left, and Kutaana began to beat his wife. She later died of multiple injuries, including a ruptured spleen, lacerated bladder, and bruised kidneys.

Kutaana told police that he had not intended to kill his wife. He was angry with her, not because she had sex with Kemjaru, but because she had not asked his permission to do so. He would have given her permission, he said, had she asked. He had done so often in the past, but he did not like her to do it without asking him.

The RCMP officer charged Kutaana with murder. This charge was later reduced to manslaughter and Kutaana was sentenced to six years' imprisonment.

There were several unusual factors in this case that made it difficult for the board to reach an appropriate decision. Kutaana barely understood English, could not speak it, and had done extremely hard time. He could not participate in any of the programs offered by the prison and had remained essentially unchanged. Because of this language barrier, no change could be hoped for in the two years remaining until his mandatory release. The main question was whether Kutaana had learned enough from his experience not to pose a threat to anyone else in his community.

Through an Inuit interpreter the board learned that Kutaana, although sorry that his wife had died, still believed that the beating he had given her had been justified. The board recognized that this was part of Kutaana's cultural background, which was not likely to change. It concluded that this attitude, combined with Kutaana's inability to participate in any alcohol program, posed a threat to any woman entering his life.

The board denied Kutaana parole because he did not meet the criteria for release, and set a review date for one year. By doing so the board hoped Kutaana would be deterred from future indiscriminate drinking and violent behaviour. He was released a year later with a special condition to report to the local RCMP detachment twice weekly for a year. Although he was instructed to abstain from alcohol, no special condition to this effect was placed on his parole certificate. The board felt that this problem could best be handled by the RCMP at the local level.

Brent Martin had three charges of assault by the time he was twenty-nine. He had a good relationship with his parents, who tended to excuse his brushes with the law as merely a result of hot temper.

Martin married at twenty-three, but was divorced after five years and three children. He had his papers as a welder and a history of continuous employment. Although he drank little during the week, he was a weekend alcoholic and occasionally used mescaline.

On the evening of the offence, he had been drinking and had taken two "hits" of mescaline. He left a bar to visit a friend who happened to be out. Backing out of the driveway, he struck a fencepost and ploughed into a newly planted garden. At that moment his friend came home and started to berate him for the damage. Martin drove the half-mile back to the bar, borrowed a shotgun from an acquaintance, returned to his friend's house, banged on the door, and fired one blast when his friend answered it.

Martin was convicted of second-degree murder and sentenced to life imprisonment. He appealed both the conviction and the sentence; the conviction was reduced to manslaughter and the sentence to eight years. He became eligible for parole after two years and eight months.

After a lengthy interview with Martin, the board was in favour of starting a release program, although not the full parole that Martin sought. Martin accepted full responsibility for his actions, and had done so since the time of arrest. He had written to the victim's parents and had reconciled with them. He had been persistent in seeking psychiatric help and had undergone a six-month program for violent offenders at the Regional Psychiatric Centre. He spoke with impressive insight regarding his former drug use, and of his determination to change his lifestyle on release. He volunteered that this would mean cutting off old acquaintances and finding new leisure-time activities. The board was satisfied that a four-month program of unescorted temporary absences of twenty-four hours a month to visit his parents posed no danger to the community. Following satisfactory completion of this UTA program, full parole was to go into effect.

Yvan Poulin, sixty-four, was the sixth child in a family of thirteen children born in rural Quebec. When he was five, he moved with his family to the United States, remaining there until he was fourteen. At that time he moved back to Montreal to work and to live with a married sister.

Poulin's record began at the age of sixteen with auto theft, and continued on and off with a variety of property offences for the next forty years. He served three federal sentences, four provincial sentences, moved solely in criminal circles, and was well known to local police.

On the evening of his last offence, he was drinking in a bar where his girlfriend was working. Her ex-husband dropped by, and words were exchanged between him and Poulin. Poulin went to the adjoining dining-room, took a knife from a table, and stabbed the victim twice, fatally wounding him.

He was charged by the police with first-degree murder. The

charge was reduced by the Crown prosecutor to manslaughter, and Poulin was sentenced to two years. He became eligible for parole eight months later, with a mandatory supervision date sixteen months after the start of sentence.

The board rejected his application for parole, despite his plea that he had finally learned his lesson. There was no evidence that Poulin had made any effort to change the attitudes that had kept him coming into prison at regular intervals throughout his life, and the board doubted, in fact, if this was possible. Although it was not the board's place to take into account the sentence given, the fact remained that Poulin had served eight months only for the taking of another's life, most of it in a minimum-security institution.

In this chapter I've tried to clear up some of the widespread public confusion about "life" sentences, as well as illustrate the fact that the range of sentencing imposed in crimes that involve the killing of another person is wide.

What emerges from an examination of this aspect of our criminal justice system is the difference between the system as it is and as how we imagine it to be. Justice is seldom meted out in a level-handed way, if it's meted out at all. Perhaps it's not the community that is drifting away from law. It is the law that is drifting away from the community.

11   *Native Criminal, White Man's Law*

The native peoples of Canada have a living standard that belongs to the Third World, yet every day they rub shoulders with one of the richest and most leisured of modern societies. Immigrants from all over the world have come here and eventually joined the mainstream, while the majority of the original lords of our land live in city ghettos and marginal reserves. The number of natives in prison reflects this bitterly ironic situation.

Just as confidently as one can predict that one is unlikely to run into a native person on the tennis courts of Toronto's Granite Club, or in the lounge of Queen's University faculty club, or in the dining-room of the Vancouver Club, so can one predict that wherever there's a prison in Canada the number of native inmates will be grossly out of proportion to their overall population.

Natives — by which I mean status and non-status Indians, Métis, and Inuit — comprise only 2 percent of Canada's population, but they constitute almost 10 percent of the total federal prison population. In the prairie region, natives make up about 5 percent of the general population and 32.7 percent of the inmate population. The figures for the Pacific region are lower, but they still remain disproportionately high; natives comprise 13.5 percent of the prison population compared with 5 percent of the overall population. On a national average, 74.1 percent of natives in prison are North American Indian, 23.3 percent Métis, and 2.4 percent Inuit.

The terrible situation in Manitoba and Saskatchewan has not improved whatsoever in the last decade, despite the efforts of some native organizations to reclaim the souls of their people from the corrosive effects of white colonization. Native people, who make up 6 percent and 7 percent respectively of Manitoba's and Saskatchewan's populations, constitute 46 percent and 60 percent of all prison admissions in those provinces. Researcher John Hylton found that status Indians are twenty-five times more likely to be admitted to a provincial jail than white males, while non-status male Indians and Métis are eight times more likely to be admitted. If we consider only the population over fifteen years of age — the population eligible to be admitted to provincial correctional centres in Saskatchewan — then male status Indians are thirty-seven times more likely to be admitted, and non-status Indians and Métis twelve times more likely, than white males.

The figures for the number of Indian women who are locked up every year are even more shocking. A status Indian woman is 131 times more likely to be admitted to prison than a white woman, and a non-status or Métis woman twenty-eight times more likely to be admitted. Can anyone seriously propose that native Indian women as a group are 131 times more criminal than white women? Perhaps some are 131 times more frustrated, more desperate, more angry, more frightened — for good reason. Sixty percent more native babies die in their first year than white babies, and the rate of suicide among native teenagers is six times the national rate. If you are a native Indian mother, the chance of your children being taken away by a white welfare agency is five times higher than it is for white mothers.

When I started working with the parole board in the prairies, I was unaware of these wretched statistics. I gradually became exposed to the extent of this tragedy as one native after another, usually with a background of unbelievable deprivation, applied for parole. I found these hearings difficult and disturbing. As a parole decision-maker, I needed to be able to understand the native inmate's family and social background, and the community to which he would return, just as I did for a white inmate. In fact, it was sometimes more important to have a realistic picture of the native's community simply because so many of them are small, and their law-abiding citizens, particularly the elderly, are reluctant to receive lawbreakers back into the community. Of all native Indian offenders in federal prisons, 78 percent come from towns of fewer than ten thousand. Forty-three percent come from towns of fewer than one hundred, isolated situations that you couldn't call communities.

I had been on several reserves, but these were located close to big towns or cities, and the men there made a good living fishing or working as loggers. Their children went to the local high school and sometimes on to university. The people on these reserves were proud and independent; their highly developed moral codes and their complicated kinship systems had remained intact.

I had never been on a reserve that was sealed up by ice for nearly half the year, or on one that had no economic base, or any access to an economic base. Nor had I ever been on a reserve where the traditional hunting, trapping, and fishing are the sole male occupations and the only source of food and revenue, and where English is virtually unknown.

When I found myself sitting opposite Samuel Grey Hawk, or Amos Morning Cloud, or Joseph Brave Bear, or when I caught the shy, uncertain eyes of a Cree-speaking teenager from the far North attempting to follow, through an interpreter, our ritualistic procedures and answer our thoroughly white, thoroughly middle-class questions, I felt a little like a fraud. It seemed incalculably unfair that these men had the misfortune to have to depend on the decisions of people who might as well have come from another planet, as far as similarities in culture and lifestyle were concerned. All I could do was try my best to make a fair decision, but trying to do one's professional best is not a substitute for knowledge and hard facts when a decision regarding retention in, or release from, prison is being made.

My sense of fumbling in the dark was heightened when interviewing the inmate. So often his life, noted in the official reports, was a sordid, tragic tale of family violence, sudden death and abandonment, illness and agency intervention. Then I would be confronted by a slight, shy youth who blushed when he was spoken to, and spoke so little and so softly as to be barely understood. Or he might be a man in his thirties or forties, polite with a modest, self-effacing air, and an anxious half-smile. Occasionally he would be a great ox of a man, handsome as the very devil, proud as Lucifer, and so filled with pain and anger that it thickened the air around him.

Almost all the board's questions were laced with values that were alien to native inmates. A job, we'd say: do you have a job? There would be a silence, a long silence, for no one on the reserve had ever had a job. Well, what will you do all day? We would wait, and then the answer would come back: There were always many things to do, and always friends to visit. Things to do, such as? A long wait, and then, through the interpreter: "Work on the trapline with my father." What about the future? we'd ask. What are your plans for the future? Again, a long silence. The concept of "future" was unknown. Often their languages have no word for it.

Sometimes the inmate was ready to go out, and if he was from a city, we would release him. Another inmate, just as ready, would be denied release simply because he was from a community in the far North with no supports available to him — not only no work, but also no self-help group of former alcoholics, no local hospital with a mental health program, no drug counsellors, no sex-offender programs. And in recent years, the Correctional Service Canada budget for the parole service in the North across Canada has been slashed, so that inmates who are slated to return to isolated communities are often hundreds of miles away from parole service supervision.

It is no favour to an inmate to release him into a situation that increases his chance of failing to fit back into society. Among other things, if he fails on parole he can lose, through a parole board vote, part or all of his earned remission, that is, the one-third of his original sentence that he normally would not have had to serve. If he has committed and been convicted of another offence, he will start to serve his new sentence only after he has finished serving that one-third.

Lack of community support has substantially reduced the number of natives released on full parole and automatically increased the number of natives who were kept in prison until their mandatory supervision dates. For instance, as of the year ending May, 1988, only 10.2 percent of native offenders had been granted full parole, while full parole had been granted to 23.9 percent of all other inmates.

Perhaps there only seemed to be no supports in northern native communities because the parole board and the parole service lacked sufficient knowledge of what was informally available in terms of community mechanisms for controlling, healing, or reconciling.

I came to realize that the languages, the geography, and the culture of the North are so different from those of the South, that the solutions for the release of native offenders from the North lay in the North, under some form of "native justice". I say this reluctantly, because I believe that the greater the number of separate structures created exclusively for native people, the greater the tendency for the current status quo to be maintained. Nevertheless, the creation of a separate native parole board seems essential if the current inequities are to be eliminated.

Lesley Cochrane was known as a "good lad" on the reserve, but suddenly in his nineteenth year he shot two people, and contributed to the death of his friend.

Cochrane's personal history was chaotic, like that of so many inmates, native and non-native, in federal penitentiaries. He was born to a twenty-year-old single Cree woman in Reliance in the Northwest Territories. His mother already had three children, and went on to have six, some by different fathers. Cochrane's father was unknown. When he was three, he was abandoned by his mother, and went to live at Dawson Landing with his grandfather, a responsible and kindly gentleman, who raised him.

A parole service report described the reserve where Cochrane grew up as poor, with no gardens or lawns or streets, just a scattering of dilapidated wooden houses connected by a network of paths that wandered across the fields, which were dustbowls in summer and bogs in winter. Most of the residents were elderly, the majority of young people having drifted south.

Although Cochrane did well at the town school to which he was bused daily, he started rebelling against his grandfather's careful, sober ways as he approached his teens. At the age of twelve he started sniffing glue, but stopped after a friend died from inhaling paint thinner. At fourteen, he quit school despite good grades and took to hanging around the reserve and drinking beer. When his grandfather was hospitalized with tuberculosis, Cochrane was left to fend for himself.

At seventeen, following a brawl with some white youths in Fort Resolution, he was given three months for assault causing bodily harm. When he was incarcerated in the local community correctional centre, he found that everyone there was either Indian or Métis. By eighteen, Cochrane, who had no employable skills and had never held any sort of job, was a powerfully built man with a reputation for being shy, always quiet and rather passive, even when under the influence.

On the night of the offence he and two friends had been drinking since early evening when they left the reserve to go into town, using an old jalopy that had neither insurance nor licence plates. They parked the car in town, and walked to a local hall where a dance was being held. There they were stopped at the door by a twenty-two-year-old white man who told them that no one who had been drinking was allowed in.

Cochrane and his friends felt they were being rejected for being native, and refused to accept the man's repeated assurance that it was because they'd obviously been drinking. A scuffle followed, the police were called, and Cochrane and his friends were told by the police to leave.

As they drove back to the reserve, Cochrane appeared to his friends to have "gone crazy"; he was pounding on the car and cursing. After they returned to the reserve, Cochrane took his grandfather's shotgun, loaded it over the protests of two friends, James Star and Francis Finley, and drove back alone to the dance hall. Star and Finley had the use of another car and raced in behind Cochrane to stop him.

Cochrane slammed the car across the sidewalk and stumbled to the dance hall, waving the shotgun and shouting. Star and Finley followed. Nobody is quite certain what happened then, except that a young couple came out of the hall just as Cochrane was attempting to go in. At the same moment the police officers who had told Cochrane to leave town pulled up outside the hall and ordered him to drop his gun. Cochrane turned around and seemed to be confused. Star snatched at the rifle, a police officer shot Star, and the shotgun, still in Cochrane's hand, went off, wounding the young woman and her boyfriend, who were pressed back against the porch wall.

Star died two hours later. Apparently, he had simply tried to get the gun away from Cochrane. Star was the youngest of four brothers and the third one to die. One had been stabbed to death in a brawl four years earlier, and the other had hanged himself the previous year in a provincial jail at the age of nineteen.

The young man who had had the misfortune to leave the hall as Cochrane arrived recovered from his injuries, but the girl's face was severely disfigured by scattered shot. Cochrane received a total of six years for wounding with intent and assault causing bodily harm. He had served two and a half years when he applied for day parole.

The board was faced with a strong and healthy twenty-two-year-old native with an above-average IQ that had tested at 115, no work history, virtually no work skills, no family support, and a propensity for violence when drinking that could result in murder.

The single insight that Cochrane had gained from incarceration was, to him, the astonishing revelation that he was not a member of an inferior race, that he was not some sort of third-class human being, but that he was a member of a proud race and a unique culture, with its own rich history and traditions.

By taking a Native Brotherhood course, he had for the first time in his life learned something of his people's past. For the first time he was exposed to the richness of native symbolism, and for the first time he was encouraged, in a systematic, constructive way to understand what it meant to be native.

Had Cochrane's lack of knowledge regarding his cultural and historic roots contributed to his explosion of aggression? Was historical and cultural knowledge relevant to Cochrane's ability to manage his life in future as a stable, law-abiding citizen? Did it have real psychological value, or was this whole "brotherhood" approach a bit of a "gaff", as inmates call a scam? At first I was unsure.

Cochrane's release plan was solid. He planned to go to the Grierson Centre in Edmonton, and to take the alcohol-treatment program at Poundmaker Lodge, a first-class native-run alcohol-treatment centre, and as we were satisfied that he met all other conditions, we let him go. He did not have any job prospects, but then he never had.

Cochrane said one thing to the board that has stuck with me, in a voice so low that I could hardly hear, "When I came in here I was acting like an animal. I shamed my race." I'd never heard any white inmate say he'd shamed his race, and God knows enough of them did. Cochrane's remorse at bringing disgrace upon the race whose values and traditions he now knew and respected led me to believe in the possibility that profound personal change could evolve from cultural awareness.

Francis Grimard was born on the Fisher River Reserve, Manitoba. He did not know his father, who was reputed to have been an extremely violent man who died in a house fire when Grimard was a few months old. There were five children in the family, and some time after the father's death the mother moved with the children to South Indian Lake where she had formed a common-law relationship. Four more children were born of this union, two of whom died in infancy.

When he was ten, Grimard's mother was killed in a car accident, and he was placed under the care of the Children's Services. He was placed in a white foster home outside Winnipeg, until the age of fourteen when he committed a break-and-enter and was sent to a boys' correctional school in Utah. There were few, if any, facilities for delinquent boys in the western provinces and placing these children in detention homes in the United States was common practice. At sixteen he was returned to Winnipeg, where he passed through a series of unworkable foster home placements. On his eighteenth birthday, he was taken to court without notice, informed that he was now an adult, that he was no longer under Children's Services, and was free to go on his own.

Grimard found himself literally dumped on the street, entirely without resources. One of his former foster parents informed him that he was from South Indian Lake, and eventually he made his way back, stealing as he went for bus fares and food. On arriving at the reserve he found that everyone in his family had disappeared. He was befriended by a sixty-seven-year-old woman who had known his grandmother.

That first evening Grimard went out with a couple of youths of his own age, started drinking, smoked some marijuana, returned to the woman's house alone, and attempted to rape her.

The woman remained calm, and her testimony in court stated that she did not feel her life was threatened, that while attempting to rape her Grimard had "cried a lot" and "seemed a little crazy".

When Grimard came to his senses in the morning the woman told him that she had phoned the RCMP. Grimard waited for the police to arrive, pleaded guilty in court, and was sentenced to four years for attempted rape.

We saw Grimard at his full parole date, after he had served sixteen months. Immediately after incarceration, he had applied for admittance to the sex-offender program at the Regional Psychiatric Centre at Saskatoon, but was still on the waiting-list. However, we had one psychiatric report and one psychological report. Both stated that Grimard was "simply the product of a disturbed childhood". He was not a sex offender as such: he would not benefit from such a program, nor did he have any of the characteristics of a violent offender. He harboured deep feelings of inferiority and loneliness, and lacked any sense of self-worth. Despite his disrupted upbringing, he was "sensitive, tender-minded, and very conscious of right and wrong".

During his time in prison, Grimard had become involved in a native life-skills program. He spent his mornings in school upgrading himself academically, and the evenings doing carving and ceramics, learning about native symbols in art, watching video programs on native culture, and learning about the history of his race.

More articulate than Lesley Cochrane, he said that he had spent most of his life in non-native homes and had never felt he really belonged. The native life-skills program had come as a profound shock to him. After three days, he said, he looked in the mirror and saw himself clearly for the first time. "My God," he said to himself, "I am an Indian!"

"I felt good about it," he said. "I knew I was an Indian, but I never really *felt* it. Like it was something I didn't want to think about. Like. . . . " His voice faded out. There was a long silence.

"Like what?" I asked quietly.

"Like I was an animal," he said. He fell silent again. Then he said "That's what one of my foster mothers would say when she was mad with me. She'd yell 'You little Indian animal.'"

The board could not consider a release on such a serious, bizarre offence without Grimard receiving some intensive psychological counselling, and without the board having further assurance that the likelihood of any recurrence was low, if not non-existent.

Grimard accepted our decision and said he'd like some counselling, but that it would have to be with someone from the Allied Indian Métis Society (AIMS) or from the Native Brotherhood. He was adamant that he would not go to the "regular guy" (the prison's white psychologist). I asked him why.

"Why?" he said. "Because now I know I am an Indian and that is where my spiritual life is."

In the last decade there has been a great expansion in the number of cultural programs and courses available to natives in prison. In the last three years, this has been accompanied by a major shift in the attitude of Correctional Service Canada towards programs designed to give natives the confidence that comes from a personal and cultural sense of identity.

For instance, each penitentiary in British Columbia now has its own sweat lodge. The sweat lodge is a central part of native spirituality. The lodge itself is an igloo-shaped building of (preferably) willow branches woven together in such a way that the space is dark and air-tight. In the centre is a fire on which are placed up to thirty-four rocks. The men participating strip to their underwear and form a "sacred circle" around this fire for the purposes of praying, and of cleansing the mind, spirit, and body.

The sweat lodges are usually run by the same native teachers who run the prison's drug- and alcohol-abuse programs, or by band elders who come in for special ceremonies. These lodges must be respected by CSC personnel, who have also been instructed not to touch or search the men's "medicine bundles" unless there is a substantial reason for doing so and unless an elder is also present. A "medicine bundle" is a collection of personal sacred objects, and could include such things as an eagle feather, a stone, a sprig of herbs, or sweetgrass.

Natives now have their own drug- and alcohol-abuse programs in most penitentiaries, and some institutions have their own social and cultural development officers, who are CSC employees. Much of the counselling that is offered by AIMS, or Nechi (a prairies organization that trains substance-abuse counsellors), or the Native Brotherhood, is done in a traditional way, in a circle, with a "talking stick" passed from hand to hand. Each circle member takes his turn in holding the stick (which is simply a stick of any wood) and saying whatever is on his mind or in his heart. This sharing of feelings is no easy thing for most natives; many of them have been institutionalized since childhood and trained to smother their feelings in order to conform and survive. First they were in a residential school, then in a series of white foster homes, then various correctional centres, and finally in a penitentiary.

What the long-term results of these self-help programs will be no one knows, but in the short term they are highly successful in dealing with drug and alcohol dependency programs, as well as with violence and other forms of anti-social behaviour. And they provide an excellent structure for involvement in related programs once an inmate is on the street.

However valuable these programs are, I reject out of hand the notion that all native crime is caused by their not knowing their cultural and historical background. There is understandable pain and confusion in not knowing one's parentage, or one's cultural roots, and deep conflict arises from being made to feel inferior as a child. All these deprivations contribute to anti-social attitudes, but none is a blanket explanation for the violence, especially against kith and kin, that permeates so many native communities.

The native crime that I saw seemed to spring out of spontaneous rage and fury, as if the heart and mind had been one long-smouldering fire that had finally been ignited into an explosion. The planning, the conspiracies, the calculated risk, the cool and deliberate scheming that characterize so many white crimes are usually absent from the average native pattern. In fact, many native crimes occur in bars, or at parties, or in the middle of the street, and often in the middle of the day when all the world is around to see. There is nothing hidden about them. The offender has no hope of avoiding detection, no hope of getting away with it. There is in much native crime a terrible element of self-destruction, a certitude of punishment to follow, a hopeless despair, and a loathing of self. No one who felt his or her life was worth living would act in this way.

I believe that while the cultural education approach seems healing and productive, it is only part of the solution, and the solution only for some. We do not say to white inmates, "Fast and pray and you'll be okay on the street," nor do most native counsellors to their charges. But sometimes such advice, intended as a recognition of the deep spirituality of the native nations, is all they have to offer on their struggling, shoestring budgets. Yet it is totally unrealistic, even discriminatory, in the face of the dehumanizing poverty and marginal existence that natives endure.

Two-thirds of all native inmates have never had a skilled job. They need money, they need work. They need to be trained in prison not only to carve and to make pottery and skin drums: they need automotive courses, small-engine courses, carpentry, welding, plumbing, electrical, and computer courses. Like it or not, ours is an industrial or even post-industrial society and natives, like everyone else, need the training to cope with it if they are going to be part of it.

In addition to direct native input at parole board hearings — if not a native parole board itself — fairness demands that trained, professional natives be employed in every type of work within the correctional system, from guards, to classification officers, wardens, parole officers, and district supervisors. Furthermore, native awareness training for all staff coming in contact with native inmates is essential if the differences between the two cultures are to be appreciated and understood. As things stand, the absence of natives in the authoritarian staff structure of our prison system helps perpetuate the exclusion of natives from the mainstream of Canadian life.

The most important perception that emerged from my hours of prison immersion was my realization of the collective human need to hurt those who have hurt society. Although we try not to be pitiless, we need victims, scapegoats for all that is wrong, in order to feel superior and in control. When society picks people as victims, it tends to gravitate towards those who irritate, who reduce our sense of well-being and heighten our sense of guilt.

Perhaps that is what this society has done with natives. I have little doubt that the disproportionately high number of natives locked up in our prisons is, in essence, nothing more than a reflection of the fact that Canadian society has found its supply of victims in the troubled and disheartened native communities that are this country's shame.

12   *The Future*

Although I started my tenure as a member of the National Parole Board of Canada knowing practically nothing about the work of the board, I left satisfied that the board does an essential and highly credible job, that the parole process is not in conflict with the sentencing process, that the policies and practices of the board do not needlessly expose the public to harm, and that the basic premise on which parole is founded — that a person can recreate his or her life — reflects the most creative and enlightened ideals of Canadian society.

I came to consider conditional release an eminently practical tool for returning inmates who have become law-abiding and self-supporting to society and to their families. I observed that those who reach this point and are kept incarcerated tend to deteriorate in their behaviour and attitudes, and come to identify more closely with the criminal element.

In *Sentencing Reform — A Canadian Approach: The Report of the Canadian Sentencing Commission, 1987* (chaired by Judge J. R. Omer Archambault of the provincial court of Saskatchewan, Prince Albert, and known as The Archambault Report), abolition of the Parole Board is recommended. I believe this is an ill-informed conclusion, based in large part on the fact that the parole structure is built on a rehabilitation model, and that prisons right now are not places of rehabilitation. While this may be true, it is the lack of rehabilitation programs that must be corrected, and not the parole system that should be elimi-

nated. If Correctional Service Canada fails to provide rehabilitative programs, and if at the same time Parliament gets rid of
the Parole Act, we might as well declare ourselves a nation
bankrupt in ethics, imagination, and creativity.

What the correctional system now provides are excellent
warehousing and containment facilities for human beings, a
sort of human pound for society's strays. Without rehabilitative
programs or parole, these pounds will become an even more
dominant feature of our society. A few of these strays are
vicious and dangerous. They are human pit bulls whose unpredictability and capacity for savagery demand long-term, perhaps even permanent, containment and separation from the rest
of society. But the majority of inmates are not violent, and
many, with appropriate training and *professional* counselling (not
just hand-holding), could rejoin society as productive citizens.

Sadly, the government of Canada — no matter which party is
in power — does not base its actions and decisions regarding
corrections policy on a set of values and principles, but rather
on politics. A clear commitment by the government to address
the problems of crime and imprisonment in an intelligent, consistent, informed manner, despite political expediency, simply
does not exist.

Where prisons are built, which has a profound effect on the
programs they can offer, and dictates whether or not an inmate
is able to sustain family relationships, is too often a political
decision. The 1988 decision to build a new prison at isolated
Renous, New Brunswick, is a prime example of such motivation. Politics also plays a role in who gets released from prison. I
do not mean that there is political interference in specific cases,
but many decisions taken by the parole board regarding major
policy directions are dictated by politics.

For instance, the decision as to whether or not the board
should be granted "gating" power to retain an inmate in prison
after he had reached his mandatory supervision date was a
political decision, arising from the government's need to appear

committed to tough measures to ensure public safety. Because the media by and large did not understand the effects of Bills C-67 and C-68, the so-called "detention legislation", the government and the solicitor-general received a great deal of favourable coverage and public support for increasing public safety. These bills actually do no such thing. They allow the parole board, after a full hearing, to hold inmates designated by correctional staff as dangerous and violent beyond their mandatory supervision date until their warrant-expiry date. Then they are released, still dangerous and still violent — perhaps more so because of their longer detention.

The creation of the twenty-five-year automatic sentence without parole for first-degree murder is a political decision with devastating consequences. This sentence, so futile in terms of rehabilitation, so costly in terms of dollars, so stupid in terms of deterrence for the individual, was made chiefly to placate various police associations and those who believe in capital punishment. Even the government recognizes the senselessness of this sentence. It has kept the back door open with the provision of a judicial review after fifteen years, thus handing the problem to the correctional service and, ultimately, to the parole board.

Politics controls who is appointed to the board. I was appointed when a Liberal government was in power: when I left the Conservatives were in office. Both governments made some excellent appointments, and both governments made some appointments that were totally irresponsible. Fortunately, for every mediocre toady appointed by the Governor-in-Council (the Cabinet) to the parole board, for every sanctimonious nincompoop, there were four or five excellent appointees.

Nonetheless, an administrative tribunal that has responsibility for the community's safety, and the power to rule on another human being's liberty, should be 100 percent first-class. The fact that all Cabinets use the board occasionally as a dumping-ground for paying off the party's old war-horses reveals the cynicism of politicians towards the non-vote-producing world of prisons and prisoners.

The knowledge that major decisions are made or not made on purely political grounds is a fact of life for those who work in corrections, but its effects are nonetheless devastating. During my years with the board, I noticed how fatigued, defeated, negative, and almost despairing many of the men and women who worked in the criminal justice system became. They had started out with optimism and energy but experience had ground them down, much as it had the inmates.

If we are going to look for ways to make positive changes, we must understand that the criminal justice system is involved in processes that often wound the human body, and always wound the human spirit. These processes start with the sense of powerlessness, the unavailability or ignorance of other alternatives, that is at the base of much anti-social or violent behaviour. From this base a powerful negativity seems to percolate through the system. Those who work in prison and around prisoners often start to feel imprisoned themselves: they can take themselves out of prison but soon find they can't take the prison out of themselves.

The entire criminal justice system, prisons in particular, have taken on some of the dimensions of a monster, huge, untouchable, and impervious to change. The dedicated classification officer or psychologist, or the humane guard, or the innovative warden all feel diminished by the behemoth of the system. When energy and sense of control, characterized by optimism and hope, are gone, a sense of powerlessness moves in.

There is a widely diffused sense akin to victimization among some who work in the correctional service. It is as if the wounds inflicted on the victim of the crime, or on the inmate as a child, or by the correctional or criminal justice systems themselves, are kept open and shared by all in different degrees. Prisons are such unnatural places that insecurities and hatreds multiply and infect every aspect of daily life.

There is so little within our correctional system to nurture the creativity needed to make our prisons more humane and more effective in rehabilitating their inmates. The desire of a warden to run a prison that does not merely deep-freeze its inmates, the efforts expended by a staff member on unpaid, after-hours counselling, the futile struggles of an inmate to get job-training or therapy are all part of a similar, unsupported, uphill battle.

It is the prison staff — the classification officers, the living unit development officers, the teaching staff, the wardens, the parole officers — who have to deal with the gap left by the absence of rehabilitation programs and must daily bear the brunt of the frustration and anger that result. No one knows better than they that alcohol and drug use are related to over 80 percent of all crimes. No one knows better than they how desperately social programs that teach simple life skills are needed. It's the prison staff who have to say a score of times each month, "You're on the waiting-list and that's the best I can do."

The staff's inability to act, to respond spontaneously and creatively to the needs of other human beings, needs that are so normal, visible, pressing, and even tragic, causes the widespread psychological fatigue, the sense of helplessness and inability to change anything that oppress the spirit of so many who work in the system.

This will not change until the people who run the system decide to stop being victims to what they have created and re-empower themselves. Deliberately and consciously, they must reclaim the system as their own and take some measure of responsibility for the negativity and lack of adequate programs.

To reduce future prison populations, we must address other needs as well. Psychiatrist Alice Miller has worked with depressed youths and young criminals for more than twenty years. She has stated that she has never worked with a person who abused others who was not himself or herself abused as a child. Dr. Karl Menninger has written about the concept of "conservation of violence": "If a child lives after being severely beaten, do you think he'll forget about it? Vengeance for that cruelty is going to come out against somebody."

The provision of good care for every child who needs it cannot be ignored if society wants to act responsibly about its own future. The failure of our society to ensure that all children receive the care, affection, and stability essential for their proper development is a major contributor to criminal behaviour in a substantial number of cases. This analysis is supported by an increasing number of academic studies, as well as by the observations of many who have worked in the treatment of children and young criminals.

If Canada had a Child Care Act that provided *all* children with the physical and psychological care they need to develop into stable and productive adults, the question of having to provide rehabilitation programs for twelve thousand inmates later on would be far less pressing. Such an act will not guarantee the safety and well-being of every child twenty-four hours a day, but it would provide eight to twelve hours of protection and care for thousands of children who are now left alone for hours at a time, or who are farmed out to inattentive, inappropriate, drunk, or sexually molesting guardians, because this standard of "care" is often all a poor family or single working parent can afford.

The proposed Child Care Act, Bill C-144 (1988), with its inadequate provision of $6.4 million for 200,000 spaces within *seven* years is now defunct. In the interim the Correctional Service budget of $759.1 million went through without a hitch, providing a clear example of where the government's priorities lie.

Few taxpayers believe any longer that the Canadian criminal justice system acts as a deterrent to the potential offender still in the community, yet they pay out over a billion dollars a year to run one of the most expensive criminal justice systems ever devised. They make no effort to improve community safety by demanding that treatment and rehabilitative facilities be available to those who need and want them.

This reluctance to adopt any sort of a proprietary attitude towards a system that is there to serve the public results from the unfortunate tradition that all our judicial and legal institutions are above criticism. My time on the board gave me a much wider perspective on the sanctity of man-made laws than I previously had. I now consider it regrettable that judicial and legal institutions should be subject to such scant and timid public scrutiny, scrutiny not necessarily for the purpose of criticism, but for the purpose of informed public discussion. If there were such scrutiny, if there were widespread, informed public discussion of our laws, and of our judicial and legal institutions, we might arrive at some consensus as to what the criminal justice system is supposed to be doing.

None of this would matter if inmates went into prison and remained there for life. Whether they ever gained employable skills or emotional and behavioural controls would be irrelevant. They would remain a threat to nobody but themselves. But former inmates return to society every day of the working week. At any time in Canada there are about 1,500 inmates on day parole staying at halfway houses, another 3,800 out on full parole and living in their own homes, and a further 2,100 out on mandatory supervision.

When inmates leave prison, they face a completely new set of problems. Their need for support and for treatment and training programs is critical. Even if a sex offender has received treatment inside prison, it cannot be assumed that he will not continue to need it on the street. Even if an addict has received alcohol or drug counselling in prison, he will continue to need supportive counselling to fight that addiction on the outside.

In the end, the entire problem of rehabilitating inmates comes down to you and me. Just as with the environmental crisis, there will be no solution until we each shoulder some of the responsibility for change.

How willing are our communities to participate in the solutions by allowing inmates to use community facilities? How much time are ordinary people willing to spend learning how the criminal justice system works? How many members of parliament will bother to understand this aspect of our society? How much responsibility are we willing to accept to see that needed treatment and rehabilitation programs are in place in prison? How much energy are we willing to expend to ensure that major decisions, such as the location of a new prison, are just and practical ones based on a philosophy and not on the garnering of votes?

Are we as a society prepared to pay in terms of money, energy, imagination, creativity, and justice to stop the generation-to-generation crime cycle, and make our communities not somewhat safer but actually safer?

If we are unwilling to accept responsibility for our society's criminals and to work at solutions that heal them and us, if we choose not to participate, not to assist and support those who work within the system now, we must be prepared to pay the appalling social consequences.

There is no other choice.

Select Bibliography

Some sources of material used in the writing of this book were:

Annual Report 1986-87, Office of the Solicitor General.

Archambault, Judge J.R. Omer. *Sentencing Reform — A Canadian Approach: Report of the Canadian Sentencing Commission, 1987.* Saskatchewan, 1987.

Badgley, Dr. Robin. *Report of the Committee on Sexual Offences Against Children and Youth.* Toronto, 1985.

Brown, J. *Stopping the Violence: Canadian Programmes for Assaultive Men.* Ottawa: National Clearing House on Family Violence, Health and Welfare, 1984.

Dreiblatt, Irwin S., Ph.D. *Issues in the Evaluation of the Sex Offender.* Washington State Psychological Meeting, May, 1982.

Final Report: Task Force on Aboriginal Peoples in Federal Corrections. National Parole Board, 1988.

Jackson, Prof. Michael. *Justice Behind the Walls: A Report of the Canadian Bar Association Committee on Imprisonment and Release.* Vancouver: UBC Law School, June, 1988.

Koenig, C. and Gariepy, L. *Canada: Life on the Outside: A Report on the Experiences of Families of Offenders from the Perspective of the Wives of Offenders.* CSC, Chilliwack, 1985.

LaPrairie, Dr. Carol Pitcher. "Selected Criminal Justice and Socio-Demographic Data on Native Women", *Canadian Journal of Criminology*. April, 1984.

Menninger, K. *Man Against Himself.* New York: Harcourt Brace, 1938.

Population Profile Report. Correction Service Canada, December, 1985.

Ross, Robert R., Ph.D. "Violence In, Violence Out: Child-Abuse and Self-Mutilation in Adolescent Offenders", *Juvenile and Family Court Journal*, University of Ottawa, August, 1980.

Steadman, Henry J. "A Situation Approach to Violence", *International Journal of Law and Psychiatry*, Vol. 5, 1982.

Personal communications and interviews included:

Sylvia Griffiths and house guests, John Howard Family House, Abbotsford; Tom Maxwell, social development officer, Matsqui Institution; John Conrad, regional director, ministry secretariat; Timothy J. Howley, forensic accountant, Peat Marwick; Insp. E. McAuley, RCMP, Vancouver; Staff Sgt. L. Richardson and Cpl. Marilyn Sims, fraud squad, Vancouver Police; Jean Sutton, National Parole Board, Ottawa; Fraser Simmons, National Parole Board, Abbotsford; Norm Fagneau and John Bissett, National Parole Board, Saskatchewan office; Audrey Thomas, Council for Adult Education, Victoria; Margit Nance, SFU, executive director Northern Justice Society; Vasa Sramek, Allied Indian and Métis Society, Mission Institution; and CSC staff, Ottawa and Abbotsford.